813 F
Faulkner, William
Twentieth century interpretations
of Light in August
Minter

DATE DUB			

GAYLORD M-2   PRINTED IN U.S.A.

TWENTIETH CENTURY
INTERPRETATIONS
OF

LIGHT IN AUGUST

TWENTIETH CENTURY
INTERPRETATIONS
OF
LIGHT
IN AUGUST

A Collection of Critical Essays

Edited by
DAVID L. MINTER

Prentice-Hall, Inc.  *Englewood Cliffs, N.J.*

A SPECTRUM BOOK

Copyright © 1969 by Prentice-Hall, Inc., Englewood Cliffs, New Jersey. A SPECTRUM BOOK. All rights reserved. No part of this book may be reproduced in any form or by any means without permission in writing from the publisher. C-13-536615-1; P-13-536607-0. *Library of Congress Catalog Card Number 76-96965.* Printed in the United States of America.

Current printing (last number):
10 9 8 7 6 5 4 3 2 1

PRENTICE-HALL INTERNATIONAL, INC. (*London*)
PRENTICE-HALL OF AUSTRALIA, PTY. LTD. (*Sydney*)
PRENTICE-HALL OF CANADA, LTD. (*Toronto*)
PRENTICE-HALL OF INDIA PRIVATE LIMITED (*New Delhi*)
PRENTICE-HALL OF JAPAN, INC. (*Tokyo*)

Contents

TWENTIETH CENTURY
INTERPRETATIONS
OF

LIGHT IN AUGUST

Introduction

by David L. Minter

In about 1914, when he was seventeen, William Faulkner began writing verse. Several of his early poems (and drawings as well) appeared, beginning in 1917, in the University of Mississippi yearbook, *Ole Miss*, and in the University newspaper, *The Mississippian*. In 1919 and 1922 single poems appeared in *The New Republic* and *The Double Dealer*, a "little magazine" based in New Orleans; and in 1924 Faulkner's first book, *The Marble Faun*, a small volume of verse, was privately printed. Attracting few sales and little attention, *The Marble Faun* taught Faulkner to speak of himself as a "failed poet" and encouraged him to turn to fiction.[1]

Faulkner's apprenticeship in fiction, prepared for as it was by his experiments with poetry, was brief, yielding but two works, *Soldiers' Pay* (1926) and *Mosquitoes* (1927). The publication of *Sartoris* in 1929 marked both his move from apprenticeship toward maturity and the emergence of his mythical kingdom, Yoknapatawpha County. "With *Soldiers' Pay* and *Mosquitoes*," Faulkner later remarked,

> I wrote for the sake of writing because it was fun. Beginning with *Sartoris* I discovered that my own little postage stamp of native soil was worth writing about and that I would never live long enough to exhaust it, and that by sublimating the actual into the apocryphal I would have complete liberty to use whatever talent I might have to its absolute top. . . . [S]o I created a cosmos of my own.[2]

The multilayered discovery that Faulkner made during the writing

---

[1] William Faulkner, "Interview with Jean Stein vanden Heuvel," in *Lion in the Garden: Interviews with William Faulkner, 1926–1962*, ed. James B. Meriwether and Michael Millgate (New York: Random House, Inc., 1968), p. 238. On Faulkner's life, see the chronology below, pp. 111–15, and Michael Millgate, *The Achievement of William Faulkner* (New York: Random House, Inc., 1966), pp. 1–57.

[2] *Ibid.*, p. 255.

1

of *Sartoris* did in fact prove inexhaustible. The publication of his last Yoknapatawpha novel, *The Reivers,* preceded his death on July 6, 1962, by but one month and two days. The discovery of Yoknapatawpha also proved immediately generative. It issued, with astonishing speed, in a series of major works. Begun in August 1931 and published in October 1932,[3] *Light in August* was the fourth and last of the important novels (the others being *The Sound and the Fury, As I Lay Dying,* and *Sanctuary*) published by Faulkner in the four years following *Sartoris.*[4] These years, years that taught Faulkner to speak of the poet as "a creature driven by demons,"[5] we have come to call "the time of genius" or "the great years."[6] In American fiction, to take an immediate context, Faulkner's first great period is now ranked with the great years of Herman Melville and the major phase of Henry James.[7]

Following a brief respite, Faulkner began, in 1936, a second period of remarkable achievement. Between October 1936 and May 1942 he published five novels, including *Absalom, Absalom!, The Hamlet,* and *Go Down, Moses.* Faulkner's third, and final, period of significant activity, which also followed a brief respite, began with *Intruder in the Dust* (1948), included *The Town* and *The Mansion,* and ended with *The Reivers* (1962). This last, and perhaps least remarkable, phase in Faulkner's literary career brought with it both public recognition, including the Nobel Prize in 1950, and critical acclaim. Both recognition and acclaim have, of course, met with resistance. But the frequent attacks of the late 20's and early 30's and the relative neglect of the

[3] *Light in August* was first published in the United States by Harrison Smith and Robert Haas (New York, 1932). The first British edition was published by Chatto & Windus Ltd. (London, 1933). Later the novel was issued by New Directions (Norfolk, Connecticut, 1947). The texts of these three editions are impressions, direct or by photo-offset, from the original plates and are reliable. Later a new edition, containing errors and changes, was published in the Modern Library series (New York, 1950). More recently Modern Library has issued a reliable text reproduced photographically from the first printing (New York, n.d.).

In the selections that follow Millgate uses one of the three early reliable editions; Abel, Brooks, Lamont, Longley, Slabey, Slatoff, and Vickery use the first (1950) Modern Library edition; and the remaining writers do not specify edition.

[4] A collection of stories, *These Thirteen* (1931), also belongs to this period.

[5] William Faulkner, "Interview with Jean Stein vanden Heuvel," p. 239.

[6] See Frederick J. Hoffman, *William Faulkner,* 2nd ed. (New York: Twayne Publishers, Inc., 1961), p. 19; Richard Chase, *The American Novel and Its Tradition* (Garden City, New York: Doubleday & Company, Inc., 1957), pp. 205–36.

[7] See Millgate, *The Achievement of William Faulkner,* pp. 42–57, 279–92.

late 30's and early 40's have, since 1946, given way to attention of very considerable magnitude.[8]

The critical consensus that proclaims Faulkner's greatness is important primarily because it enables us more adequately, if still tentatively, to define the nature and extent of his achievement—to distinguish its qualities and fix its boundaries. Less drastically experimental than *The Sound and the Fury* and *As I Lay Dying, Light in August* is more "conventional" in structure and technique and is therefore less perplexing to approach, although it clearly does not represent "a return" by Faulkner "to the traditional novel." More substantial and compelling, more clearly "a major work" than *Sartoris* or *Sanctuary, Light in August* is more fully suggestive of Faulkner's greatness.[9] In short, it is a good place for serious, inquisitive readers to begin to know the magnitude and order of Faulkner's created world and to begin to locate the critical problems appropriate to it.

The shorter excerpted statements that make up the second part of this collection present contrasting positions on those aspects of the novel that have proved most problematical—the status and significance of the major characters of each of the novel's three main strands and the roles in the novel of religion, sex, and women. The essays that constitute the first part of the collection represent a variety of approaches to the novel as a whole. Richard Chase ties *Light in August* to an American literary tradition. Michael Millgate points to basic affinities between the novel and major traditions of British and Continental fiction of the nineteenth century, affinities he sees enriching rather than compromising both the unusual emotional and moral engagement that Faulkner demands and the unconventional techniques that he employs. Cleanth Brooks sees in the pervading force of the community a clue to the novel's central structure. Darrel Abel seeks to define the nature of its fluid reality and to describe the poetic techniques used in capturing and creating that fluid reality in a literary form. Olga Vickery traces three patterns of imagery, the circle, the shadow, and the mirror, which work in the novel to

---

[8] For a discussion of the critical reception of Faulkner's fiction, see Robert Penn Warren, "Introduction: Faulkner: Past and Present," *Faulkner: A Collection of Critical Essays,* Twentieth Century Views Series (Englewood Cliffs, N. J.: Prentice-Hall, Inc., 1966), pp. 6–19. On 1946 and the publication of Malcolm Cowley's *The Portable Faulkner* as the "great watershed for Faulkner's reputation in the United States," see p. 10.

[9] See Michael Millgate, *William Faulkner,* Evergreen Pilot Books (New York: Grove Press, Inc., 1961), p. 44; and Olga W. Vickery in this collection.

relate isolated individual consciousnesses to one another and to a shared public world and which work, too, to suggest how reason and imagination together integrate individual need and communal need, private realm and public arena. Such variety in itself testifies to the rich complexity of *Light in August*.

II

Among those of Faulkner's qualities that have impressed all of his better readers are the fecundity of his imagination, the range of his compassion, and the reach of his courage as artist. Not only within his fictional kingdom of Yoknapatawpha County, population 15,611, area 2400 square miles, "William Faulkner, sole owner and proprietor," [10] but within his individual novels as well, we find an "abundance of representation," scores of compelling, unforgettable characters, and an "abundance of narrative incident," a wealth of action in language.[11] Faulkner possessed, in short, fecundity of the rare sort that we associate in the novel with Balzac, Dickens, and James. Commensurate with his fecundity was the range of his interest and compassion. Reaching beyond those he grandly termed "the unvanquished," those who remain impervious even to final defeat, his interest and compassion touch the terrible, like Percy Grimm of *Light in August*'s brutal climax, and the small, those "who stand a little in the background," [12] like the furniture repairer and dealer of *Light in August*'s last chapter. Equal, too, to Faulkner's fecundity was the reach of his courage as artist, his willingness, or as some would have it, his compulsion, to expose and explore every aspect of each of his novelistic worlds.

Such courage, at least in Faulkner's case, was not without its dangers: on occasion the difficulties we encounter stem less from profundity of vision than "from the fact that his mind is so astonishingly energetic, his sensibility so vividly aroused by all the issues present to his mind, that he is . . . leaping from one [possibility] to the other in excited discovery." [13] But Faulkner's world is finally an ordered world, and

---

[10] Malcolm Cowley, "Introduction," *The Portable Faulkner*, The Viking Portable Library (New York: The Viking Press, 1946), p. 5.

[11] Irving Howe, *William Faulkner: A Critical Study* (New York: Random House, Inc., 1952), p. 154; and Michael Millgate in this collection.

[12] Cowley, "Introduction," *The Portable Faulkner*, p. 20.

[13] Alfred Kazin, "Faulkner in His Fury," *The Inmost Leaf: A Selection of Essays* (New York: Harcourt, Brace and Company, 1955), pp. 266–68.

it is, accordingly, big rather than swollen with significance. Faulkner possessed to remarkable degree the coherence of imagination that marks novelists of the first rank: "the ability to sustain details in so long and dynamic a single period that they finally compose a single order of progression." [14] In his determination to move toward the largest possible extension of meaning, Faulkner frequently employs big, familiar devices and motifs—most noticeably, in *Light in August,* the odyssey motif and elements of the Passion story.[15] But his world is a world of the immediate and the actual, of small, specific sounds and colors, through which he endows even the most familiar and universal of conventions with a local habitation. Albert Camus, one of Faulkner's early admirers, once remarked that what he liked most about Southern fiction was "the dust and the heat." [16] In Faulkner's world "the actual," the land and the ways of the land that he knew, its dust, its heat, its humor, not only precede and prepare for but become (in Faulkner's term, are sublimated into) "the apocryphal."

Faulkner's determination to expose every aspect of each of his imagined worlds meant, among other things, that his fictions frequently would defy even such familiar and useful distinctions as that between comic and tragic modes. In *Light in August,* even more, say, than in the predominantly comic *As I Lay Dying* or the predominantly tragic *Absalom, Absalom!,* the two mingle. To Cleanth Brooks, the mode of the novel is finally "that of comedy"; to Olga Vickery and John L. Longley, it is finally tragedy.[17] But to these and all other

[14] *Ibid.,* p. 268. See Darrel Abel, Cleanth Brooks, Norman Holmes Pearson, and Olga W. Vickery in this collection.

[15] On the odyssey motif, see Michael Millgate in this collection; and Alfred Kazin's splendid essay, "The Stillness of *Light in August*," which, because it has been several times reprinted and is available in Robert Penn Warren, ed., *Faulkner: A Collection of Critical Essays,* Twentieth Century Views Series (Englewood Cliffs, N. J.: Prentice-Hall, Inc., 1966), pp. 147–62, has not been reprinted here. On Faulkner's use of the Passion story, see Faulkner and Brooks in this collection and C. Hugh Holman, "The Unity of Faulkner's *Light in August*," *PMLA,* LXXIII (March, 1958), 155–66. On Faulkner's use of such motifs, compare his description of the inception of *As I Lay Dying*: "I simply imagined a group of people and subjected them to the simple universal natural catastrophes which are flood and fire with a simple natural motive to give direction to their progress." ("Interview with Jean Stein vanden Heuvel," p. 244.)

[16] Quoted in Kazin, "The Stillness of *Light in August*," p. 149.

[17] See Brooks, Vickery, and Longley in this collection. John L. Longley's fine discussion of "Joe Christmas: the Hero in the Modern World" has not been reprinted in full in this collection only because it is readily available in Robert Penn Warren, ed., *Faulkner: A Collection of Critical Essays,* Twentieth Century Views Series (Englewood Cliffs, N. J.: Prentice-Hall, Inc., 1966), pp. 163–74.

careful readers it is clear that in this several-stranded story the two modes are mixed. The novel begins with Lena Grove and ends with Lena, her child, and Byron Bunch. In this strand, in which Lucas Burch is a supporting character, a villain to be precise, the mode is comedy. And in this strand the comic heroine, Lena Grove, is dominant, and the comic hero, Byron Bunch, subordinate. Between the first and last chapters (the novel's framing chapters, and the only chapters in which Lena is dominant), we encounter two other stories: first, at considerable length, the story of Joe Christmas, in which Doc Hines and Mr. McEachern, together with Lucas Burch and Percy Grimm, are subordinate villains, and Joanna Burden something of a subordinate heroine, and in which the mode is tragedy; and second, more briefly, the story of Gail Hightower, in which the comic and the tragic very much mingle. All of which is to say, first, that the novel's dominant hero and heroine pull it in different directions (which in turn is to suggest why, appropriately, they never meet), and second, that, in addition to being counterpointed, the hero's tragic story and the heroine's comic story are interlaced by the story of Gail Hightower.

Joe Christmas' desperate, violent search for "peace"—"That was all I wanted," he says[18]—his search for a sense of his own identity and a sense of place in his world, is a "tragic and essentially modern story." The journey, the frantic circling, of this "doomed, deracinated, terribly alone" man is not merely futile but extravagantly destructive. In clear juxtaposition is the "steady imperturbable onward linear progress" of Lena Grove, through whose life, and through the birth of whose child, the "barren and ruined" (p. 385) world of the novel is partially renewed. Gail Hightower, who witnesses the terrible death of Joe Christmas and attends the calm childbearing of Lena Grove, is by the conjunction of the two, by the suffering of the one and the renewing generation of the other, moved "from rigidity into life." [19] The issue that has troubled even the most careful readers of *Light in August* is the relation of the novel's three strands and particularly the success of Hightower's unifying strand, the dynamics and the significance, the how and the so what, of Hightower's renewal.[20]

[18] *Light in August* (New York: Harrison Smith and Robert Haas, 1932), p. 313. All page references in the text of this introduction are to this edition of *Light in August*.

[19] Millgate, *William Faulkner,* pp. 44–49. On Joe Christmas' isolation, compare Alfred Kazin's discussion in "The Stillness of *Light in August,*" p. 151, of him as "the most solitary character in American fiction."

[20] See Howe, *William Faulkner,* pp. 148–49. Even Kazin, in "The Stillness of

The link between Lena Grove and Joe Christmas that provides a basis for their unwitting cooperation in Gail Hightower's emergence resembles the link Hannah Arendt has described between the saint and the criminal: "the one [the saint] being for, the other [the criminal] against, all men," she writes, both "remain outside the pale of human intercourse and are, politically [and otherwise], marginal figures." [21] At first glance, Joe Christmas may seem a pure instance of the criminal. He commits, after all, among other things, a terrible murder. Several critics, including Malcolm Cowley, one of Faulkner's best readers, have linked Joe Christmas and Popeye, the grotesque villain of *Sanctuary,* as willing agents, dehumanized, deliberate extenders, of destruction.[22] The far simpler Lena Grove might seem at first to support such a view: to confirm that it is her hand that is for and Joe Christmas' that is against all men. But Lena Grove is after all too finely, even too traditionally, drawn a comic heroine in the pastoral mode to be in any simple sense a saint. Furthermore, in keeping with Faulkner's superbly controlled compulsion toward complexity, Lena, as an unwed mother in a traditional society, is something of an outcast as well as something of a saint.[23]

Allied as she is with everything that is permanent and enduring, with everything that is natural, simple, certain, Lena is able to comprehend the whole of her world with "a single glance all-embracing, swift, innocent and profound" (p. 5); she is at home in it endlessly, from day to dark and dark to day again. A man with no authentic name and with none to come, Joe Christmas is, in Melville's term an "isolato." Whereas Lena moves slowly, purposefully across the face of her world, Joe Christmas circles furiously, ever hesitating and alone, forever gray and indefinite as a shadow. Whereas Lena's linear odyssey brings forth life, Joe Christmas' circular flight ends in death. Yet, just as Lena is outcast as well as saint, Joe Christmas is something more than criminal; at least in his last moments, as he lies on the floor conscious, unmoving, accepting death, he becomes an emblem of terrible and yet hopeful sacrifice.

Light in August," p. 148, is troubled by Faulkner's "attempt to will his painful material into a kind of harmony that it does not really possess."

[21] Hannah Arendt, *The Human Condition* (Chicago: University of Chicago Press, 1958), p. 180. Compare R. W. B. Lewis, *The Picaresque Saint: Representative Figures in Contemporary Fiction* (Philadelphia: J. B. Lippincott Company, 1959).

[22] Cowley, "Introduction," *The Portable Faulkner,* p. 15.

[23] See p. 4, where we learn that to her brother Lena is "a whore," and compare pp. 7–8.

He just lay there, with his eyes open and empty of everything save consciousness, and with something, a shadow, about his mouth. For a long moment he looked up at them with peaceful and unfathomable and unbearable eyes. Then his face, body, all, seemed to collapse, to fall in upon itself, and from out the slashed garments about his hips and loins the pent black blood seemed to rush like a released breath. It seemed to rush out of his pale body like the rush of sparks from a rising rocket; upon that black blast the man seemed to rise soaring into their memories forever and ever. They are not to lose it, in whatever peaceful valleys, beside whatever placid and reassuring streams of old age, in the mirroring faces of whatever children they will contemplate old disasters and newer hopes. It will be there, musing, quiet, steadfast, not fading and not particularly threatful, but of itself alone serene, of itself alone triumphant. (pp. 439–40)

The strange story of Joe Christmas demands of us disturbing flexibility. For it requires that we entertain a disquieting possibility: that in a world which so easily accommodates itself to the cruelty of a sheriff who beats defenseless others, to "the insensitive, life-denying rigidity" of McEachern, and to the "principled inhumanity" of Doc Hines and Percy Grimm,[24] that in a world in which absurdity and injustice so resoundingly reside, the furious and confused response of Joe Christmas, no less than the calm and purposeful response of Lena Grove, is necessary and even heroic. Since we see Lena primarily as a pastoral creature, and not as an outcast, and since we associate her not only with everything that is natural, simple, fertile, but also with that triumph of artifice, Keats' bride of quietness and slow time, we know that she must endure.[25] Similarly, since we see Joe Christmas as isolated and hollow, and even, in clothes and manner, as strangely urban, since we associate him with everything that is barren and artificial, we know that he must die. "Something is going to happen to me," we hear him quietly think; "I am going to do something" (p. 97; compare p. 110). We know, in short, that it is Joe Christmas and not Lena Grove whom some terrible fatality awaits. But *Light in August* nonetheless stands among those works of modern literature, including the entire literature of hipsterism, in which we see, and must ourselves accommodate, a blurring of the line between saint and criminal, suppliant and murderer.[26]

[24] Millgate, *William Faulkner*, p. 49. See, too, Millgate's discussion of tension in *Light in August* between masculine adherence to "clear-cut patterns of crime and punishment" and feminine "tendency to blur" those patterns (p. 46).
[25] See Darrel Abel and Norman Holmes Pearson in this collection.
[26] See the works cited in note 20 above.

The movement of Joe Christmas' story is from what he has done (his killing of Joanna Burden), first, to the history lying behind and illuminating what he has done, back to what he has done, and finally to what happens to him. What Faulkner achieves by thus defying, almost obliterating, the distinction between passivity and activity, between what the world does to shape Joe Christmas and what he does to shape his world, between everything that happens to Joe (injustice, violence, and death) and every act that he commits, is to suggest that in the case of Joe Christmas the two are not only inter-related but inseparable. The death Joe Christmas meets at the hands of Percy Grimm is prefigured in the death he inflicts on Joanna Burden. The pistol that Joanna Burden holds, the pistol that misfires, delaying the death of Joe Christmas, later has its dual counterpart in the scene of Joe Christmas' death—first in the pistol that Joe Christmas holds but does not fire and second in the pistol that Percy Grimm holds and empties into the body of Joe Christmas, thus completing the destruction that Joanna Burden attempted and that, long before her, Hines and McEachern began. Similarly, the razor with which Joe Christmas grotesquely kills Joanna Burden has its counterpart in the bloody knife Percy Grimm wields in mutilation. The death Joe Christmas meets is thus anticipated by, is thus implicit in, the death he inflicts.

What is most strikingly clear in the relation between the death Joe Christmas inflicts and the death he suffers is true, too, of his whole life. At virtually every point he is both active and passive, both agent and victim. In describing and attempting to account for the final, futile run that culminates in Joe Christmas' death, Gavin Stevens sees and articulates in racial terms a fundamental conflict within Joe Christmas: [27]

". . . his blood would not be quiet, let him save it. It would not be either one or the other and let his body save itself. Because the black blood drove him first to the Negro cabin. And then the white blood drove him out of there, as it was the black blood which snatched up the pistol and the white blood which would not let him fire it. And it was the white blood which sent him to the minister, which rising in him for the last and final time, sent him against all reason and all reality, into the embrace of a chimera, a blind faith in something read in a printed Book. Then I believe that the white blood deserted him for the moment. Just a second, a flicker, allowing the black to rise in its final moment and make him turn upon that on which he had postulated his hope of salvation.

[27] See the discussions of Joe Christmas as hero in this collection.

It was the black blood which swept him by his own desire beyond the aid
of any man, swept him up into that ecstasy out of a black jungle where
life has already ceased before the heart stops and death is desire and
fulfillment. And then the black blood failed him again, as it must have
in crises all his life. He did not kill the minister. He merely struck him
with the pistol and ran on and crouched behind that table and defied
the black blood for the last time, as he had been defying it for thirty
years. He crouched behind that overturned table and let them shoot him
to death, with that loaded and unfired pistol in his hand." (pp. 424–25)

Some such conflict is indeed the basic conflict not only within Joe
Christmas but within his world. But it is a conflict rather between
life and death than between "white blood" and "black blood." The
two figures representing opposite poles in the world of *Light in August,*
Lena Grove, the source of life, and Percy Grimm, the instrument of
death, are both white.[28] What Faulkner does in *Light in August* is to
revise and extend, through poetic context and action, the conflict described, but miscast, by Stevens.

The struggle Joe Christmas wages with his world is a struggle for
peace and life, for repose and creation, against fury and death. His
defeat, though neither simple nor full, is certain in part because he
lives in a world he never made, a world too large and too hostile
for him to conquer or even withstand. He is, in short, overmatched.
A part of what we see in him, therefore, is man as victim. His suffering,
at once concentrated, large, and representative, is in part imposed
and inflicted. To Joe Christmas as victim, pity is the proper response;
to him we say what Gail Hightower says: "Poor man. Poor mankind"
(p. 93). But, as John L. Longley has suggested, we feel, before Joe
Christmas' terrible ordeal, not only pity but terror.[29] And it is this
that suggests that Joe Christmas is more than either victim or villain,
that he is tragic hero as well, that in him Faulkner renders not merely
individual man as enemy and victim of man but individual man as
enemy and victim of himself. What we learn in the story of Joe Christmas' early years is how, in the orphanage and in the home of the
McEacherns, he has become, *in part,* an ally of his world against
himself. The ambiguity that is his heritage and his identity, his de-
fining quality, touches more than race, parentage, and place; it touches

---

[28] Note that Stevens assumes what in the novel remains in doubt: that Joe Christmas is part Negro. Note, too, how small a role Negroes, apart from whites' preoccupation with them, actually play in the novel.

[29] See John L. Longley in this collection; see, too, the fuller piece by Longley as
cited in note 16 above.

his basic disposition toward life. What we see in Joe Christmas' circular flight, in his attitude toward women, in his fear of progeny, and in his failure, by firing at Percy Grimm, to resist death, is the deep division within him between the forces of life and the forces of death. Both the Christmas who resists and flees death and the Christmas who serves and welcomes death are present to the end. Joe Christmas the ally of death not only refuses to oppose Percy Grimm, that ally of racism, perverse religion, militarism, and fear of sex; he even embraces the death Percy Grimm offers as peace, as release from the pain, ambiguity, and suffering that are his life.[30] But the Joe Christmas who flees and defies death, too, is present to the end. It is he who refuses to permit his perverted self to kill Hightower; it is he who stills the hand so long turned against man and life, the hand that would destroy, in Hightower, the one man so moved by his ordeal as again to become, despite fear, an ally (albeit an ineffectual ally) of life. And it is this Christmas who endures the death his other self embraces, who accepts it, who suffers it, not as release but as means of becoming, for all who see him, an emblem of sacrifice.[31] It is because of the continuing presence of this self, which is at the end "of itself alone serene, of itself alone triumphant," that Joe Christmas is able to speak to us not merely of "old disasters" but of "newer hopes" (p. 440).

The shadows and the grayness that we associate with Joe Christmas point to the division within him between the forces of death, the impulse toward it, the yearning to inflict and to suffer it, and the forces of life, the impulse toward peace, not as escape but as repose and generation. The shadows and the grayness accordingly suggest that to the end Joe Christmas belongs neither to Lena's world nor to Hines's, McEachern's, and Grimm's, but to both. His triumph is that, despite everything that is done to him, he remains in part dedicated to life. That dedication we see, moreover, not only in the suffer-

---

[30] On Percy Grimm, see William Faulkner, Letter to Malcolm Cowley [September 20, 1945], *The Faulkner-Cowley File: Letters and Memories, 1944-1962*, ed. Malcolm Cowley (New York: The Viking Press, 1966), p. 32. Faulkner describes Grimm as a "Fascist galahad who saved the white race by murdering Christmas." "I didn't realize," Faulkner adds, "until after Hitler got into the newspapers that I had created a Nazi before he did." See Olga Vickery and Maxwell Geismar in this collection; and Ilse D. Lind, "The Calvinistic Burden of *Light in August*," *New England Quarterly*, XXX (1957), 307-29.

[31] Compare Millgate, *William Faulkner*, p. 47: "The main function of the much-discussed Christ-imagery which clusters around Christmas, especially at the moment of his death, is not to make him a 'Christ-figure'—an unnecessarily portentous term —but to underline his role as a sacrificial victim."

ing that defines his acceptance of death but also in the fury and violence that ironically define and undermine his doomed search for peace in life.

Because Joe Christmas finally speaks complexly of "newer hopes" as well as more simply of "old disasters," he can join Lena Grove as occasion and instigator of Hightower's emergence into life. In Hightower's preoccupation with the past we see not mere withdrawal from life but denial of it. We see, that is, something very close to the tension and struggle that are Joe Christmas' drama. By choosing to live in the non-world of his empty illusions, Hightower has become, for his wife in her Memphis hotel room and for himself in his morbid mausoleum, an agent of death. For him vision has been illusion, not dream, an instrument of death rather than of life. His story in *Light in August*, however, is the story of his reluctant move toward reentering life. Before we witness his futile effort to save Joe Christmas, we see him successfully deliver Lena's child. When we move from Chapter 19, which centers on the death of Joe Christmas, to Chapter 20, which culminates in Hightower's vision, we move to a style that begins in elegy and moves toward epiphany. Through attending Lena in the birth of her child and Joe Christmas in the ordeal of his death, Gail Hightower is renewed. He perceives the primal hope which Lena represents in her "tranquil obedience to . . . the good earth['s]" command that she renew and replenish her "barren and ruined" world (pp. 384–85). And he apprehends the complex hope that Joe Christmas bespeaks. Prepared as he is by the logic of his own life, by his own deep ambivalence toward life, Hightower is in fact enabled not only to apprehend but to appropriate that hope, to make it the very substance of his final vision. The fruit of his renewal, the sign of his emergence "from rigidity to life," is his move from vision as illusion to vision as illumination. After he has given up his distortions of the past, after he has admitted the truth regarding his grandfather's death and has accepted responsibility for his wife's death, he discovers in the relation he discerns between Joe Christmas and Percy Grimm that the struggle between life and death is a struggle waged not only among men but within man. It is only after we have shared Hightower's vision that we fully understand the hope as well as the disaster that defines the drama of Joe Christmas.

Hightower's illusion, the illusion he comes so reluctantly to see as illusion, is in one of its aspects a denial of life. But it is in another aspect a token of his desire that death, if it must triumph over life, triumph with the sound of drums and the clash of swords, not with the screech of a man whose sleep has been disturbed by chicken thieves and with the blast of a fowling piece, that least discriminate and most inglorious of weapons. What Hightower finally sees—and what through him we see—is that the struggle between life and death is, not merely in the case of Joe Christmas but characteristically in his world, a struggle in which glory and degradation are profoundly mixed and are so precisely because man is deeply ambivalent toward life itself. But Hightower sees, too, that death's triumph is neither simple nor full; he sees that through continued refusal simply to choose death, refusal that defies the force of everything his world does to him, Joe Christmas is enabled to express hope as well as disaster. In his continued, though mixed, allegiance to life, maintained as it is despite the violence that besets, partially corrupts, and finally destroys him, Joe Christmas becomes an emblem, not of mere terror, but of terrible hope.

Light in August ends with Lena, her child, and her would-be lover and husband. The rich styles of the nineteenth and twentieth chapters give way to the calm, detached, colloquial, humorous voice of a furniture repairer and dealer, a simple man in bed telling his wife the story of what he has seen on his travels. But the vitality and endurance of Lena surely are not, in any simple way, commensurate with the terrible stories of Joe Christmas and Gail Hightower. Lena endures, and her endurance permits her to end the novel she has begun. But she does not prevail. Her tranquillity lasts to the end—her voice remains to the last scene "quiet, tranquil, stubborn" (p. 18). But it does not bring tranquillity to its world. Lena remains fascinated with life, wondering at how a body gets around. But her repose and fascination are weaknesses as well as strengths. They are born of her energy and vitality, her instinctive engagement with and love of life. But they are limited by her obliviousness to the suffering of Joe Christmas, whose last home she inherits but whom she somehow essentially cannot meet, and to the suffering of Gail Hightower, upon whom she depends but whom she never understands. She endures as easily as she does only by being inured to the hardship and privation of her own life and only by remaining impervious to the sufferings of those destroyed by a world in which she lives and thrives. Her comic story, centering on the birth of her child, a birth that in many details parallels what we know about the birth of Joe Christmas, thus frames the very different stories that dominate *Light in August*. But it does not balance the bleakness of the stories juxtaposed to it. For the final meaning of *Light in August* we must look beyond the simple

story of Lena, first, to the complex stories of Gail Hightower and
Joe Christmas, whose lives, save for the meaning they yield, are
altogether grim and barren. And we must also look to the relations
that the novel establishes among its three principal characters rather
than to the very different relations that it depicts as informing the
lives those characters live. In brief, we must look for meaning to the
novel as a formal whole. In the life the novel renders, Lena Grove
touches and alters but never comprehends Gail Hightower, and she
remains almost totally oblivious to Joe Christmas. Only through the
novel's structure does the inadequate hope of Lena's comic story en-
close and embrace the terrible hope of the tragic stories of Joe Christmas and Gail Hightower.

III

Two very different works published in 1942, Maxwell Geismar's
Writers in Crisis and Alfred Kazin's *On Native Grounds*, seriously
challenged Faulkner's claim to our attention. To Geismar, Faulkner's
career reflected increasing fascination with "the perverse and the
pathological." Further, Faulkner's tendency to see "humanity only
in terms of its aberrations" seemed to Geismar to culminate in the
displayed "variety of perversions which the writer contrives for his
characters" in *Light in August*. As though to complement Geismar's
work, Kazin attacked not the stuff but the style and form of Faulkner's
work, describing Faulkner's complicated techniques as springing rather
"from an obscure and profligate confusion . . . than from an elaborate and coherent aim." [32] Increasingly, however, we have come to
see in Faulkner's work, not simple fascination with the perverse and
the pathological, but complex devotion to the "poet's . . . duty" as
he saw and defined it: the duty to write of "the human heart in conflict with itself," of man torn and debased by hate, greed, and fear,
yet "capable of compassion and sacrifice and endurance." [33] Gradually,
too, as Kazin's own career suggests, we have made peace with Faulkner's "solitary" style and strange formal experiments.[34] For we have

[32] Maxwell Geismar, *Writers in Crisis: The American Novel, 1925–1940* (Boston:
Houghton Mifflin Company, 1942), pp. 167–68. Alfred Kazin, *On Native Grounds:
An Interpretation of Modern American Prose Literature* (New York: Reynal and
Hitchcock, 1942), p. 457.
[33] William Faulkner, "Nobel Prize Address," *Faulkner Reader* (New York: Random House, Inc., 1954), pp. 3–4.
[34] Compare Kazin, *On Native Grounds*, pp. 453–68; "Faulkner in His Fury," pp.

come to see what Conrad Aiken saw quite early: that the "uncompromising and almost hypnotic zeal" with which Faulkner insists on his style is a token of his dedication to his art, and that, if we are to understand Faulkner, we must understand the "functional reason and necessity" of the elements and structure of his style[35]—of his seemingly indiscriminate fondness for big words like *imponderable*, smaller ones like *outrage* and *amaze*, and strange ones like *avatar* and *apotheosis*,[36] and of his seemingly indefensible use of sentences that seem "needlessly involved" and "perversely thick with parentheses, [and] even with parentheses within parentheses." [37]

Full understanding of the significance of Faulkner's famous "Protestant" rhetoric must await fuller knowledge of the literary models and oral traditions that helped inspire it. But we may begin to understand its purpose by noting that Faulkner's most famous and problematical words are used in relation "to individuals of every type and in every class" and in relation "to houses, hills, roads, [and] dogs" as well. "These words are not merely interjections"; they are essential. They create the dominant "atmosphere" in which Faulkner's characters, "Negro . . . white, Southern . . . Northern, old settlers . . . new exploiters," move.[38] What most of Faulkner's characters and all of his readers essentially must feel, sooner or later in one way or another, is "outrage" and "fury" before the terrible violence and injustice that foil man's efforts to remake and perfect the living state of his world, and "outrage" and "astonishment" before the constant motion that defies full, final understanding of the why and wherefore of that violence, injustice, and failure. The structure as well as the elements, the form as well as the content, of Faulkner's "strangely fluid and slippery and heavily mannered prose"—those "queer sentences" that at first so often seem "monsters of grammar or awkwardness"—prove in the end "extraordinarily effective" in rendering a basically violent

---

257–73; and "The Stillness of *Light in August*," pp. 147–62. And compare Clifton Fadiman, "Faulkner, Extra-Special, Double-Distilled," *William Faulkner: A Collection of Critical Essays*, Twentieth Century Views Series, ed. Robert Penn Warren (Englewood Cliffs, N. J.: Prentice-Hall, Inc., 1966), pp. 289–90; Conrad Aiken, "William Faulkner" [1939], *A Reviewer's ABC: Collected Criticism of Conrad Aiken* (New York: Meridian Books, Inc., 1958), pp. 201–2; and Cowley, "Introduction," *The Portable Faulkner*, pp. 3–4.

[35] Aiken, "William Faulkner," pp. 200, 202.
[36] For more complete lists, see Kazin, "Faulkner in His Fury," p. 259; and Cowley, "Introduction," *The Portable Faulkner*, pp. 3–4.
[37] Kazin, "Faulkner in His Fury," p. 259.
[38] *Ibid.*, pp. 262–63.

and endlessly problematical reality.[39] For Faulkner's style forces us to stand before and enter his created world in the only attitude proper to it, an attitude, moreover, that is close to one we see again and again displayed in his characters' disposition toward life. Before the violence and injustice that torture Faulkner's world we must feel not only outrage and fury but also astonishment and bafflement, and we must do so precisely because the source and the end of that violence and injustice are problematical.

It was through his "peculiar" style and his "elaborate method[s] of deliberately withheld meaning, of progressive and partial and delayed disclosure" that Faulkner found in art an adequate mistress to his terrible, complex, and inexhaustible vision of outraged and baffled man, man who knows himself immersed and committed yet ambivalent toward his terrible world, who knows, too, that his efforts to find and perfect the life he seeks must fail and that his efforts to understand both his world and his failure must forever remain imperfect. In the "fierceness and openness" of the prose of *Light in August* we see reflected Faulkner's sense of outrage at the implications of his vision.[40] But in the novel's calm stress upon the beatitude of its own formal achievement, its stress upon its triumph in creating in art relations and fulfillment missed and lost in life, we see reflected Faulkner's sense of pride that at least in art, in the anguish of imaginative contemplation and the labor of aesthetic translation, man triumphs over the terrible failures that define his life.

[39] Aiken, "William Faulkner," pp. 202–3.
[40] *Ibid.*, pp. 200–203; and Kazin, "Faulkner in His Fury," p. 265.

PART ONE

Interpretations

Faulkner's *Light in August*

by *Richard Chase*

There could hardly be a more characteristically American novel than *Light in August*—with its realism; its loose structure; its few characters who though vividly presented are never quite convincingly related to each other; its tendency to become a romance by taking on a legendary quality and by alternating violent melodramatic actions with comic interludes and scenes of pastoral idyl; its concern with the isolated self; its awareness of contradictions, racial and other; its symbolism of light and dark. Generally speaking, *Light in August* is in these respects akin to books apparently as diverse as *The Prairie, The House of the Seven Gables, Moby Dick, The Grandissimes,* and *Huckleberry Finn*, not to mention *Uncle Tom's Cabin* and many others, including such novels of more recent vintage as Robert Penn Warren's *Night Rider* and Ralph Ellison's *Invisible Man*.

In *Light in August* things are perceived in space rather than temporally as they are in *The Sound and the Fury*. Except for the Reverend Hightower, one of Faulkner's characters who are ruined by time, no one is particularly aware of time; and the surviving, enduring character, Lena Grove, lives in a timeless realm which seems to be at once eternity and the present moment. The Mississippi landscape spreads out before us and the faculty of vision becomes very important as we are shown the town of Jefferson, the houses of Hightower and Miss Burden, or the smoke on the horizon as Miss Burden's house burns. There is much use of the painter's art (even the sculptor's, as when Faulkner makes a wagon slowly passing through the countryside look like part of a frieze, or a seated person—Lena Grove or Hightower—resemble a statue). The art style is not cubist or otherwise modernist as it sometimes is in Faulkner's writing (*Pylon*, for example); it is serene, harmonious, and always aware, even in the midst of dark and violent actions, of a luminousness and spatial harmony that suggest an eternal order.

A simple and somewhat disconnected story emerges from the "abundance of representation," which, as Irving Howe correctly says, constitutes the splendor of *Light in August*. Lena Grove, a poor and ignorant farm girl from Alabama, painfully wends her way into northern Mississippi in pursuit of Lucas Burch, with whose child she is pregnant. Hearing that her ne'er-do-well lover has got a job at a sawmill near Jefferson, she goes there and finds Byron Bunch and Joe Christmas. But Burch has left; as the story goes on, Lena has her child and at the end is still on the road, an example apparently of perpetual motion. Now she is accompanied not by Burch but by Bunch; which one accompanies her she seems to regard as a matter of indifference.

Meanwhile in a long and exhaustive flash-back we are told the history of Joe Christmas, an orphan and (as everyone including himself assumes) part Negro. We are told how Christmas murders Miss Burden, a descendant of New England abolitionists, and how he is caught, escapes, and is finally murdered himself in the Reverend Hightower's kitchen by Percy Grimm. We are also told a good deal about the life of Hightower, particularly how he ruined his career and lost his wife because of his fantasy of identification with his Confederate grandfather, an officer in the army who had been killed in Jefferson during the Civil War. As the story unfolds, Hightower is now an old man isolated from the world, but before he dies he gets more or less involved with Lena and Joe Christmas and serves rather loosely as the unifying figure and center of intelligence of the last sections of the novel. There are thus three separate strands of narrative in *Light in August*, each having its central character. The book makes a kind of triptych.

Lena Grove is one of those intensely female females we meet in Faulkner's books, like Eula Varner in *The Hamlet*. A somewhat bovine earth mother, she has all those womanly qualities which, as Faulkner likes to point out, baffle, fascinate, outrage, and finally defeat men. According to Faulkner's gynecological demonology (it constitutes a sort of Mississippi Manichaeism) men are more interesting and valuable than women but the dark or Satanic principle of the universe

decrees that they are the weaker sex and are doomed to be frustrated
and ephemeral. Faulkner appears to agree both with folk superstition
and Henry Adams that compared with women men are in Adams's
word "epiphenomenal."

The bovine woman brings to Faulkner's mind echoes of ancient
myth and ritual (hence the name, Lena Grove . . .) and he treats
her alternately with gravity and with a measure of humorously gran-
diose fantasy and mockery. Lena's placidity is not only that of the cow
but unmistakably that of the gods in their eternity. Hence Faulkner
has given her a ritual office by associating her with the religious procession depicted in Keats's "Ode on a Grecian Urn," a favorite poem of
Faulkner of which there are several echoes in *Light in August*. In
Lena's unvarying inner harmony (and here Faulkner is serious rather
than mocking) all opposites and disparates are reconciled or perhaps
rendered meaningless. In the words of Keats's poem, beauty is truth
and truth beauty. By implying that Lena Grove somehow symbolizes
this ideal unity Faulkner suggests no metaphysical reconciliation. He
merely praises again the quiet enduring stoicism and wisdom of the
heart which he finds among the poor whites, Negroes, and other so-
cially marginal types.

The first thing to be said about Joe Christmas is that he is not a
villain, as is sometimes thought. Nor, except in a distantly symbolic
way, is he a tragic hero or a "Christ-figure." He has many of the qualities Faulkner admires. He suffers, he is a divided man, he is marginal
and bereaved; he is "outraged." He asks merely to live, to share the
human experience, and to be an individual. Like the slave in "Red
Leaves," he "runs well"—he has in other words some power of giving
his doomed life meaning by insisting as long as he can on his right to
be human. All this outbalances his being a criminal. It even outbalances his being a murderer.

It is the custom of some traditionalist critics to say, in the words of
one of them, that "sentimentalists and sociologists are bound to regard
Christmas solely as a victim," whereas actually he is a tragic figure akin
to Oedipus. But the main difference between Joe Christmas and Oedipus (or any other tragic hero in the full classic sense) is that Christmas
really *is* a victim; he never has a chance, and a chance, or at least the
illusion of a chance, a tragic hero must have. It is true that in *The
Sound and the Fury* and perhaps elsewhere Faulkner achieves a gen-
uine tragic vision of life and evokes the profound and harmonious emotions that tragedy evokes. But on the whole his vision of things is more
akin to that of "sentimentalists and sociologists" than to that of Sopho-

cles—if by this we mean that, like many modern novelists, he takes a
rather darkly naturalistic view of things but finds a saving grace in the
simplest sentiments of men. Joe Christmas, as Faulkner presents him,
is a character conceived not in the manner of the tragedian but of the
naturalistic novelist. There is no mystery, no disastrous choice, no
noble action, no tragic recognition. Instead there are heredity, environment, neurotic causation, social maladjustment. What happens later
to Joe Christmas is made inevitable by the circumstances of his boyhood in the orphanage. In fact one may be very specific about the
origin of the train of causes. Christmas's life is given its definitive bias
by his encounter with the dietitian, described near the beginning of
Chapter 6. Hiding in a closet and eating toothpaste, he has seen the
dietitian making illicit love. When she discovers this, Christmas expects, and *desires,* to be whipped. Instead she offers him a silver dollar:

> He was waiting to get whipped and then be released. Her voice went on,
> urgent, tense, fast: "A whole dollar. See? How much you could buy.
> Some to eat every day for a week. And next month maybe I'll give you
> another one."
>   He did not move or speak. He might have been carven, as a large toy:
> small, still, round headed and round eyed, in overalls. He was still with
> astonishment, shock, outrage.

What the boy wants is recognition, acceptance as a human being, if
only through physical punishment. A whipping would establish the
passionate, human contact. Instead he is given a silver dollar, and he
sees his doom in its adamant, abstract, circular form. He has now been
given an irresistible compulsion to destroy every human relationship
that he gets involved in. And this compulsion includes the suicidal
desire to destroy himself.

Joe Christmas thus joins the long procession of isolated, doomed
heroes that begin to appear in the American novel with Brockden
Brown, Hawthorne, and Melville. This is not the place to discuss the
complex picture of Protestantism that emerges from *Light in August;*
yet one may note that in the isolation of Christmas (and others in the
book) Calvinism is still strongly felt as an influence, despite the fact
that the psychology Faulkner has applied is generally "Freudian," in
the popular behavioristic sense. Apparently nothing appears to our
American novelists to be more terrible than to have become isolated
or to have fallen victim to a cold, abstract hatred of life—nor, we must
admit, does any doom call forth a more spontaneous admiration or
require a more arduous repudiation.

But if Christmas has his American ancestors, Faulkner has also made some attempt at modernizing him by making him in effect a Conradian or postromantic, existentialist hero. The portrait of Kurtz, the ultimately lost, rootless, and alienated man in Conrad's *Heart of Darkness,* is a distant model for Christmas. The Reverend Hightower, too, is a kind of Marlow (the narrator of Conrad's story), if only in the tone of his voice and in his physical appearance ("Hightower sits again in the attitude of an Eastern idol, between his parallel arms on the armrests of the chair"). And it is clear that Faulkner has learned some of his more florid rhetoric from Conrad. The following passage might have come from the pen of either Conrad or Faulkner; it is from *Heart of Darkness*:

> And in the hush that had fallen suddenly on the whole sorrowful land, the immense wilderness, the colossal body of the fecund and mysterious life seemed to look at her, pensive, as though it had been looking at the image of its own tenebrous and passionate soul.

This sort of thing has its own rhetorical magnificence, although both Conrad and Faulkner are perhaps a little too easily moved by the fecund, the pensive and the tenebrous. And there is no doubt that these authors—melodramatists both—tend to construct a rhetoric of doom and darkness in excess of what the occasion demands.

The Reverend Hightower is one of Faulkner's best characters. He appeals to us in many ways—first and most importantly in the sad everyday conditions of his life: the decaying house with the weatherbeaten sign in front saying "Art Lessons Christmas Cards Photographs Developed"; the swivel chair in which he sits before the desk with the green shaded reading lamp as he gazes fixedly out the window; his moving colloquies with Byron Bunch, who, though his companion, is so different from him in heritage and intellect—as different as Sancho Panza is from Don Quixote (a parallel which is very much in Faulkner's mind). Only because Hightower is established in novelistic detail do we become interested in the fantastic obsession that has ruined his life. Like Quentin Compson and Horace Benbow (see *Sartoris* and *Sanctuary*), Hightower is one of Faulkner's intellectuals— he is fastidious, genteel, frightened by life. Haunted by the glory and crime of the past, he is incapable of living in the present. Like Quentin Compson he tries willfully to impose a kind of order on the irrational flow of time and nature. His view of things, however, is not metaphysical or theological like Quentin's; it is purely mythic and aesthetic, the product of a mind immersed in Keats and Tennyson. A careful reading of the pages at the end of Chapter 20 will show that Hightower does not return to his earlier Christian belief in his moment of ultimate insight before he dies. The turn of his mind is to grasp truth aesthetically; truth is for him an ecstatic perception of a supreme moment in the natural, historical order, a moment in which, to employ the Keatsian vocabulary Faulkner encourages us to use, beauty is grasped as truth and truth as beauty. Before he dies he sees the truth about himself—"I have not been clay"—which is merely a way of admitting finally that neither truth nor beauty can be perceived by the mind that remains inverted and solipsistic and denies man's common fate in nature and time. This is the truth that finally comes to Hightower; and it is what allows him to see for the first time, and pathetically for the last, the full beauty of the myth he has lived by. For a moment he can now be free, for the first time and the last. The progression of his views has thus taken him beyond his Christianity and his pure aestheticism to a full, profound, perhaps tragic naturalism (to use the word in its philosophical rather than strictly novelistic reference).

A good deal has been written about the symbolism of *Light in August,* and although much of this criticism has been predictably beside the main points, it remains true that this novel has in it a much more complicated symbolism than *The Sound and the Fury* or *As I Lay Dying.* The most obviously conscious and willed symbolism is the least successful—such as the attributes of Christ Faulkner associates with Joe Christmas; these have an artificial, inorganic, even an arty quality about them. The symbolism that seems most profoundly organic with the action and meaning of the book is that of the circle, and I would judge that, like any interesting symbol, this was half consciously intended by the author but has implications within the book of which he was probably not entirely conscious when he wrote it.

Three circles should be kept in mind; they are associated with the three main characters. Remembering the theme of solitude vs. society, alienation vs. community . . . in *As I Lay Dying,* we remember also that Faulkner spoke of Addie Bundren's aloneness as a circle that had to be violated in order to be made whole. Although this is a literary idea that Faulkner might have absorbed from many sources, among them Yeats, the symbol of the circle of selfhood may be taken as an archetype of the modern imagination, and especially wherever Puritanism has made itself felt. Lena Grove's circle, then, since she is a kind of earth goddess, is simply that of the death and renewal of nature. She is also associated with the urn of Keats's ode and the ritual procession of its encircling frieze. In the circle of her being truth and beauty are perpetually absorbed into each other. In Lena selfhood is whole; it is congruous with experience, with nature and with time.

The circle associated with Joe Christmas is the fatalistic, repetitive pattern of his life; in actual symbolization it varies from the silver dollar the dietician gives him to the pattern of his flight from the sheriff and his dogs. He wants, of course, to break out of his circle—"to define himself as human," in the words of Robert Penn Warren. Yet whenever this becomes possible, usually in relation to a woman he has become involved with, he succumbs to the irresistible compulsion to preserve his isolation. Finally, virtual suicide is the only solution. One might add that his circle is also racial; he is doomed to oscillate helplessly between the white world and the black.

If Christmas's imprisoning circle is imposed on him by circumstance, the Reverend Hightower's is imposed by himself, forged by his own intellect and neurotic fantasy. Only at the end when for a moment he is released from the isolation and stagnation of his life does the wheel that is a part of his obsessive fantasy finally spin free:

> The wheel whirls on. It is going fast and smooth now, because it is freed now of burden, of vehicle, axle, all. In the lambent suspension of August into which night is about to fully come, it seems to engender and surround itself with a faint glow like a halo. The halo is full of faces. The faces are not shaped with suffering, not shaped with anything: not horror, pain, not even reproach. They are peaceful, as though they have escaped into an apotheosis; his own is among them.

Despite the religious overtones of the language, this ultimate vision of Hightower seems to be a purely naturalistic intuition of his own solidarity with the other people he has known. It is this intuition that finally frees him.

The symbolism we have been noticing runs fairly deep, but it remains of the natural order, as, on the whole, does similar symbolism having to do with the self and its isolation in the writings of Hawthorne, Melville, and James. The specifically Christian symbolism in *Light in August* is not made deeply significant. It seems impossible to be much impressed with the fact that Faulkner calls one of his characters "Joe Christmas," and that he is thirty-three years old, has his feet votively bathed, and is in a manner crucified. The symbolism of the circle would certainly, if we had here a specifically Christian novel, include the traditional symbolism of death and the newborn spiritual life. But this central mystery of Christianity is not present. And *Light in August* reminds us that Faulkner's imagination is not characteristically stirred by incarnation, catharsis, and harmony, but rather by separation, alienation, and contradiction. If *Light in August* were a Christian novel it might use the symbolism of the book as it stands —the circle, the opposition of light and dark, and so on. But in some way it would have to employ the idea that life comes about *through* death, that in some way a new spiritual life had come to the community of Jefferson through the death of Joe Christmas. But this does not happen; there is no new life, no transfiguration anywhere that would not have occurred without Joe Christmas. There is no new religious consciousness or knowledge. In Joe Christmas we do not celebrate the death and rebirth of the hero.

Light and dark, good and evil, life and death, Eros and Thanatos are postulated in *Light in August* as eternal and autonomous contradictions. There is no possibility of absorbing and reconciling these contradictions in a whole view of life that is in any specific sense religious, or, for that matter, tragic. There are only two courses open: 1) to commit some transcendent act of horror or violence or suicide, 2) to find reattachment to the simple concrete conditions of life, through love, stoic patience, or humor, for in this way one may, as it were, temporarily step aside from the eternal contradictions in which humanity is involved and give the world the appearance of harmony.

The Shadow and the Mirror: *Light in August*

by Olga W. Vickery

Despite Faulkner's use of a clearly defined plot, *Light in August* is by no means a return to the traditional novel. Rather it constitutes his attempt to integrate certain experimental features of his earlier novels into a conventional narrative frame, thereby carrying one step further his use of structure to clarify theme. In both *The Sound and the Fury* and *As I Lay Dying* the public world serves merely as a frame for events which the reader is engaged in seeing from different perspectives. In *Light in August,* however, we are no longer concerned with examining the particular nature and limits of the individual consciousness but rather with its relation to other minds and to the public world of events, statements, and mass responses.

Because of the interpenetration and interdependence of the private and public worlds, each character is multidimensional. He is at once subject and object, observer and observed, creator and created. Thus, Joe Christmas as well as the Reverend Hightower and Joanna Burden are both self-crucified and crucified by others, both villain and victim. The interplay of these polar aspects of the human being produces much of the dramatic tension and the grotesque quality in the novel. There is a continual movement from one world to another, each with its own kind and degree of distortion. Depending upon who is acting as observer, this distortion provides a mirror image of the particular world of the observer or of the public world as represented by the town of Jefferson. In a sense, the individual and the community are obverse reflections of each other. Yet because the reflection is obverse, each fails to recognize himself, and so reacts with instinctive fear and

"The Shadow and the Mirror: Light in August." *From* The Novels of William Faulkner: A Critical Interpretation [*1959*], *rev. ed., by Olga W. Vickery (Baton Rouge: Louisiana State University Press, 1964), pp. 66–83. Reprinted with the permission of the publisher.*

anger which ultimately lead him to destroy his own image. In short, each is the victim of the other.

The nature of the private world and its relation to others is indicated by a threefold pattern of interlocking imagery—the circle, the shadow, and the mirror. All the main characters in *Light in August* are strangers to Jefferson and they remain strangers no matter how long their stay or how deep their roots. Their isolation is suggested by the image of the circle which achieves its clearest expression and greatest significance in the episode of Joe Christmas' flight and his sudden realization: "It had been a paved street, where going should be fast. It had made a circle and he is still inside of it. . . . 'And yet I have been farther in these seven days than in all the thirty years,' he thinks. 'But I have never got outside that circle.'" (296) In the midst of that jostling, noisy intercourse which is society and to which all men contribute, each is alone, unable to break through the circumference of his own circle or to admit anyone into it. Because of the solipsistic quality of the private world, each individual sees others and is himself seen as a shadow, ghostlike and unreal. Walking the streets of Jefferson, Joe Christmas, for example, looks like "a phantom, a spirit, strayed out of its own world, and lost." (99) The images of the circle and the shadow are linked in the description of Byron Bunch and Brown, passing "one another as though on opposite orbits and with an effect as of phantoms or apparitions." (386) It is Hightower, however, who extends the insight provided by these images with his recognition that other people are simply "mirrors in which he watches himself." (427)

Yet no matter how isolated and impenetrable the private world of an individual, he still has a physical and social existence in the public world which makes its demands of him. His comfort, if not his life, depends on his accepting and exemplifying in his own life those stereotypes which represent society's vision of itself and its past. And since withdrawal or rebellion are as much public acts as is affirmation, no one can escape. Society has myths not only of the hero but also of the antagonist, and it has evolved rituals to deal with each. Collectively, Jefferson is Southern, White, and Elect, qualities which have meaning only within a context which recognizes something or someone as Northern or Black or Damned. This antithesis is periodically affirmed through the sacrifice of a scapegoat who represents, in fact or popular conviction, those qualities which must be rejected if Jefferson is to maintain its self-defined character.

Miss Burden, Hightower, and Christmas serve as such scapegoats and serve willingly, almost eagerly, since they too have accepted the absolute necessity and validity of the dichotomies in whose names they are destroyed. Thus, Miss Burden, despite her birth in Jefferson, is a "Northerner" in the eyes of the town, and hence she is automatically aligned with the "Negro" and the "Damned." Hightower, on the other hand, offends not by being a Northerner but by refusing to play the role of "Reverend" in the manner established by custom and tradition. He becomes "Gail Hightower Done Damned in Jefferson." (52) This judgment is then in part justified and in part explained by the town's accusation of Hightower's unnatural relationship with a Negress. Out of this judgment his ritualistic punishment by masked men and his ostracism follow inevitably. Joe Christmas, of course, represents the third category, that of the Negro, and it is this assumption that predetermines the manner of his pursuit and lynching. But at the same time he constitutes an omnipresent threat to all categories: he cannot say with certainty whether he is Negro or white; he is a Southerner with too many Northern ideas; and he seems quite indifferent to salvation or damnation.

Accordingly, Christmas has a dual function in the novel. As an individual, he explores his own relation to the myth of the Negro, while as a part of society, he is identified with the myth. Through his oscillation between repudiation and affirmation of his black blood, he reveals his own uncertainty and his need to resolve the dilemma posed to him by the old Negro gardener: " 'You dont know what you are. And more than that, you wont never know. You'll live and you'll die and you wont never know.' " (336) He is obsessed with the idea that he must choose, yet his every action emphasizes his inability to do so. In the world of Jefferson, however, after Brown's accusation has taken root, he is treated as if he were in actual fact a Negro. The varying responses, ranging from Gavin Stevens' cool, impersonal analysis to Gail Hightower's anguished sympathy to the mob's violence, are directed at the concept of the Negro with which he is identified. Inescapably Joe is forced into the ritual of pursuit and lynching performed almost casually by a society which has been elaborating it for generations.

The basis of this pattern is Jefferson's conviction that the individual can only become a member of society by permitting himself to be classified according to race, color, geographic origin, and so on. Created by man, these categories become creators of man insofar as they establish social identification as the necessary prerequisite to human existence. The sheer weight of generations, each in its turn conforming to and therefore affirming this process of public labelling, establishes the labels not only as a matter of tradition but as a kind of revealed truth. What starts as a verbal pattern of classification thus becomes a social order not to be challenged or changed. And what starts as a category becomes a myth, for certainly the word "Negro" is a compressed myth just as the stock response to that word is a compressed ritual. The result is that men like Joe Christmas or Velery Bon, who can neither fit nor be fitted into these categories, are either sacrificed to or driven out of the society whose cherished beliefs they threaten.

Certainly there is no one set of categories which can claim Christmas or be claimed by him. He is indeed the "disaccommodated man," with "something definitely rootless about him, as though no town nor city was his, no street, no walls, no square of earth his home." (27) Yet he cannot ignore the concept of race which assigns men to one of two separate worlds, each with its traditions and modes of thinking and acting. The irony of Joe's position is that what seems to be a choice is in reality a delusion: Negro or white—to choose one is to affirm the existence of the other. His awareness of this dichotomy makes him take up the role of antagonist in all situations. In the presence of whites he becomes Negro; among Negroes he feels himself to be white. The result is that series of tensions and conflicts for which he himself is at least partly responsible. The Joe Christmas who is finally lynched as "Negro" is the joint creation of his private world and of the larger public universe.

In this respect Mrs. Hines's account of his birth becomes significant, for it reveals that Joe is born into a myth created for him by others. Since Millie's pregnancy is considered an unforgivable sin by Hines, he looks for a scapegoat who will bear the guilt and punishment. By calling her lover a "nigger," he can transform a commonplace seduction into the horror of miscegenation. That is his justification, moral and religious, for the brutally inhuman treatment of his daughter, her lover, and her child. His reasons for regarding Christmas with malevolence and hatred remain personal, but his actions and statements help formulate that confused and violent myth which is Joe's particular agony. His brooding watchfulness having isolated Joe from the other children at the orphanage, Hines then provides the three year old with an explanation: " 'Why dont you play with them other children like you used to? . . . Is it because they call you nigger?' " (335) The awareness of something strange or different about Joe is thus simultaneously impressed on Joe and on others.

The identification of Joe with Negro receives additional and unexpected support from the dietitian. Surprised in the midst of her clandestine love affair, she lashes out at Joe calling him a "little rat" and a "little nigger bastard." In the days of frenzied uncertainty and fear which follow, she links the carelessly spoken invective with Hines's attitudes and with the meaningless taunts of the children. Though she had never considered Joe to be a Negro, "she believed that she had, had known it all the while, because it seemed so right: he would not only be removed; he would be punished for having given her terror and worry." (113) At cross purposes, each speaking a strange, private language, and each motivated by personal reasons, the dietitian and Hines, nevertheless, combine to extend and intensify Joe's awareness of himself as a different kind of being and to force the matron to act on the assumption that he is indeed a Negro.

Although the "taint" of Negro blood is never revealed to McEachern, Joe himself is imbued with its possibility. For a time, however, it lies quiescent in his consciousness while he endeavors to assimilate yet another aspect of his life. To the social pattern of black and white, the implications of which he is yet to realize, is added the religious pattern of the elect and the damned. His vague, emotional response to God is replaced by the creed and discipline of a particular church. And the spiritual relationship of father and son is submerged in an intricate and deadly game of good and evil, reward and punishment. McEachern's religious discipline is accepted eagerly by Joe because it makes his life completely predictable, relieving him of the necessity for self-judgment and responsibility. Accordingly, he rejects Mrs. McEachern's awkward and uncertain attempts to establish a more purely human relationship with him.

Ultimately, however, he seeks and finds such a relationship in his love for Bobbie, the waitress. It is this love which prompts him to rebel against McEachern's Calvinistic ritual of confession and penance and to resist the customary punishment which McEachern seeks to inflict on him at the dance. But this achievement is short-lived, for Bobbie's later shrieks of rage signal the destruction of the last of Joe's natural, spontaneous emotions. Her betrayal, which impels him into the long, lonely street of his life, is not only sexual but religious and racial, for all three are involved in the idea of miscegenation into which their affair is suddenly transformed. So long as their affair proves satisfactory and trouble free, Bobbie simply ignores Joe's confession that " 'I think I got some nigger blood in me.' " (171) In a moment of crisis, however, and in order to save herself, she, like the dietitian, finds it convenient not only to believe but to act upon that belief. All blame, all possible punishment is shifted to Joe as "Negro" who significantly enough has himself provided the material for this accusation. Suddenly conscious of her white blood, Bobbie has no compunctions about abandoning a "nigger" whom she had naively mistaken for a white man nor about watching that "nigger" beaten senseless by her friends.

The beating establishes the antithesis of black and white in Joe's own physical experience and thereby intensifies his awareness of it. His life becomes a series of episodes in which he provokes racial violence from Negro and white alike, a violence which constitutes an almost joyful affirmation of the Negro-white pattern in which both Joe and his opponents are trapped. That someone could simply ignore that pattern fills him with an indignant amazement and outrage. He beats the prostitute who refuses to be horrified by his Negro blood, thus forcing her to initiate that ritual of violence which he expects. His reaction is understandable, for her indifference challenges the validity of the premise on which he has built his whole life. Whether or not he himself is a Negro may remain in doubt, but that there is something called Negro which demands certain attitudes and actions on the part of all white people must not be denied.

During his relationship with Joanna Burden, Joe's preoccupation with such categories becomes especially acute since he recognizes the same obsession in her. In fact, her concern with racial, geographical, and religious myths serves as a complement and antithesis to his own. Not even their frenzied and insatiable love-making can destroy their ingrained awareness of what each believes the other to represent. While her body surrenders completely to his, Joanna still mutters "Negro! Negro! Negro!" And Joe, on his way to her bedroom, still pauses to smash the dishes of food prepared by the white woman and left for him in the kitchen. Thus, even miscegenation is powerless to erase their concern with racial differences and indeed serves only to intensify it.

Joe's wild hope, as he holds her letter in his hand, that they can escape from their own preconceptions into a world where " 'She is still she and I am still I' " (238) is doomed from its very inception. For what he visualizes is a return to the natural world where the only meaningful categories are male and female and the only meaningful relationship is sexual. But Joanna, her physical need for him exhausted, demands of him that choice which he has spent his whole life evading. She insists that he ignore his uncertainty and accept once and for all the role of Negro as modified by the North together with that of repentant sinner. The violence between them is inevitable, but significantly it is both impersonal and unimpassioned. Joanna's act of raising the pistol and Joe's use of the razor are both projected as shadows against the wall—phantom weapons directed at phantom opponents. For each sees embodied in the other that racial myth which has dominated their lives and which they must destroy if they are to be free.

Yet in the very act of gaining his freedom, Joe loses it. The act of murder leaves him vulnerable to society's judgments and actions. The fire at Miss Burden's and her decapitated body generate a tension in the milling crowd which needs only the proper spark to explode it into violence. That spark is supplied by Brown, a man whose parentage is as obscure as Joe's own. The pattern made familiar by Hines, the dietitian, and Bobbie is repeated as the cry of "Negro" and the suggestion of miscegenation channel the restless and undirected energy of the observers away from the accuser. Three times Brown repeats " 'Accuse the white man and let the nigger go free' " until the crowd grasps the significance of that contrast and prepares itself for action. Once he pronounces the word "Negro," the actual guilt of Joe Christmas, the circumstances, and the motivation, all become irrelevant, for the connection between "Negro" and "murder" is part of the public myth. At the same time Joanna Burden loses all individuality, becoming simply a white woman and hence an innocent victim who must be avenged. Accusation, conviction, and punishment constitute a single simultaneous belief-act as "Joe, the son of Joe" becomes Joe, the son of a Negro.

The compelling nature of the pattern evoked by Brown is indicated by the fact that no one thinks to question his premise. The mob is, of course, wholly absorbed in the idea of revenge, but even those who sympathize with Joe never doubt that he is a Negro. Though he has ample evidence of Brown's character, Byron still takes his word and in his turn convinces Hightower. The intense shock felt by the latter is occasioned by his sickening realization that a public myth is once more demanding its victim, that the ritualistic sequence of the chase, the pursuit, and the final immolation is now inevitable. Even the cosmopolitan Gavin Stevens, with his Harvard and Heidelberg studies behind him, is not able to see Joe Christmas except through a filter of preconceptions. Though he recognizes that Hines is quite mad, he, nevertheless, accepts his contention that Joe's father was actually a Negro. More important: despite his disinterested rationalism and objectivity, he assigns definite though arbitrary moral values to black and white blood, claiming that it was the former which made Joe strike Hightower and the latter which enabled him to die heroically.

As these stock reactions and attitudes crystallize in Jefferson, Joe Christmas himself is able if only temporarily to escape their coercive pressure. At the outset he is still sufficiently obsessed with the fictions he has spent his life affirming through endless challenges to pause in a Negro church. Standing in the pulpit and cursing God, he assumes, possibly in his own mind and certainly in the minds of the congregation, the terrifying form of anti-Christ. But the body's need for food and rest erases all the illusions that the mind creates and perpetuates. The stage beyond, where even food becomes unnecessary, gives to Christmas the human dignity all his violence could not seize. For the first time, he sees his life not in terms of "black" and "white" but simply of the human race. Inevitably his new found awareness of himself as man causes him to be rejected by both the Negroes and the whites. Negro fear is balanced by white outrage at the fact that " 'He never acted like either a nigger or a white man. That was it. That was what made the folks so mad.' " (306)

Ironically, as Christmas transcends the categories of black and white and of good and evil, thus resolving his own personal dilemma, he is once more forced to exemplify them in the sequence of flight and pursuit, capture and death, begun by his own act of murder but given shape by Brown's accusation of "nigger." Dazedly he half-comprehends that he has given himself up to the public world by his act and that he can no longer refuse the role it has given him to play. Since he is a "nigger" murderer, each gesture, even each emotion which he is permitted to feel, is already established. Sardonically he reflects on his unsuccessful attempts to give himself up: " 'Like there is a rule to catch me by, and to capture me that way would not be like the rule says.' " (294) As Christmas recognizes the inevitability of this pattern and of his own part in it, he visualizes himself sinking "at last into the black abyss which had been waiting, trying, for thirty years to drown him and into which now and at last he had actually entered, bearing now upon his ankles the definite and ineradicable gauge of its upward moving." (289) Significantly, he becomes aware of the borrowed shoes as a symbol of his acceptance of "the black abyss" only when he is in the wagon on his way to Mottstown to give himself up and thus to assume the role of Negro which Jefferson has prepared for him.

It is, then, as "Negro" that Christmas is lynched in a scene that echoes and intensifies all the earlier acts of his life. In the "cloistral dimness" of Hightower's house Christmas resembles "a vengeful and furious god pronouncing a doom" (406) on the men whose "faces seemed to glare with bodiless suspension as though from haloes." (405)

Saints and sinners, the elect and the damned, the victim and the persecutors become strangely confused with one another. Through Percy Grimm, the "young priest" of the occasion, the elect and white of Jefferson castrate and slay the Negro according to ancient custom, but instead of purification, they are left with a sense of their own guilt and self-doubt. Through his castration, Christmas finally does escape society's categories. Having made him a "Negro" in order to crucify him, society, by its own passion for affirming the reality of its myths in actual living experience, in the end explodes both those myths and the categories out of which they were evolved. It is no longer the Negro murderer or even Joe Christmas but simply "the man" who rises "soaring into their memories forever and ever." (407)

In the moment of Christmas' death, then, there occurs a final violent fusion of the public and private myths of the "Negro," a fusion developing out of the interaction of these myths as charted in the actual chronological sequence of the novel. Moreover, in the process of unfolding this interaction the chronological sequence has shown the gradual identification of the individual, Joe Christmas, with this public myth. Through Joanna Burden and Gail Hightower that identification is given historical perspective, not only because they themselves are conscious of the historical origins of the particular myths which dominate Joe Christmas and themselves alike, but because they have virtually stopped living in the public world where their beliefs might be modified by further interaction. At the same time they represent the two remaining categories, one geographical and the other religious, in terms of which the South establishes its identity. The Negro, the Yankee, the Apostate—these are the key figures in a society which defines itself by exclusion.

Like Joe Christmas, Joanna Burden presents an obverse reflection of one aspect of the South. For though she is excluded from the community as a Northerner, she too is obsessed with the myth of the Negro. Despite the apparently irreconcilable opposition of their attitudes which led them to actual war, both North and South are concerned with the problem of the Negro, a concern which gives form and substance to a concept but which takes no cognizance of individuals as individuals. In both, this concept, bolstered by the legends of history as seen from their own particular perspective, engenders a set pattern of beliefs and actions. Eventually, these acts and beliefs involving the "Negro" are transformed into a kind of religion, a distorted version of Calvinism in which black and white replace or are identified with evil and good. Each holding this extreme view, Joanna Burden, the scion of New England, is scarcely distinguishable from McEachern or even Hines.

Joanna's increasing awareness of this myth parallels Joe's, though without his tormenting uncertainty as to his own relationship to it. As a child, she simply accepts that fact that certain people have darker skins than her own. But this innocence or naïveté is not permitted to continue. Her father, Nathaniel Burden, slowly transforms the physical black and white she sees into a moral and religious order. She is made aware of "Negro" " 'not as people, but as a thing, a shadow in which [she] lived, we lived, all white people, all other people.' " (221) The shadow becomes a "black cross" to which she is a martyr, a phantom priestess immolating herself on a phantom altar. Consequently, her whole life is devoted to perpetuating and giving substance to a metaphor: " 'You must struggle, rise. But in order to rise, you must raise the shadow with you.' " (222)

To this belief in her martyrdom, Joanna Burden sacrifices all her natural impulses, thereby creating a bifurcated individual. Thus, Joe sees her as "a dual personality: the one the woman at first sight of whom in the lifted candle . . . there had opened before him, instantaneous as a landscape in a lightningflash, a horizon of physical security and adultery if not pleasure; the other the mantrained muscles and the mantrained habit of thinking born of heritage and environment with which he had to fight up to the final instant." (205) His entrance into her life signals an overt conflict between these two aspects of her being. The sex-starved body conquers for a time "the mantrained habit of thinking" and expresses itself in a desperate and imperious need to experience every possible sensation and every possible emotion that physical love can suggest. Acting out of a world of fantasies, she quickly passes "through every avatar of a woman in love": (226) the lover's pursuit, secret trysts, baseless accusations and jealousy, seduction, and even rape.

Yet even in the midst of these exaggerated manifestations of her long suppressed desires, she is not entirely free of her intellectual heritage. She can only seek to postpone its mastery over her: " 'Don't make me have to pray yet. Dear God, let me be damned a little longer, a little while.' " (231) The implicit identification of sex with sin prepares the way for the corruption of her relationship with Joe and for her own final perversion in which he ceases to be the means of satisfying her physical demands and comes to symbolize the sexual superstitions associated with the Negro. In this last phase, she is not having intercourse with a man but with an image of her own creation, with the idea of "Negro" for which she has given up her life. Accordingly, she emerges from the affair with her instincts once more subdued and with her obsessions once more crystallized and intensified.

No longer driven by her desire to sin, Joanna is left free to brood over the fact that she has sinned. In retrospect she naturally sees all the facets of her relationship with Christmas in the light of her old "man-trained habits of thinking" and the result is a reaffirmation of Calvinism and rededication of herself to the black cross. Nor can she leave Christmas alone, for he is the Negro, the symbol of her responsibility, her sin and damnation, and most important, her salvation. Her pleading, bribes, and threats are her attempt to make him translate into living flesh and act her concept of the Negro. He is to ignore his own uncertainty, admit his black blood, his sinfulness, and his dependence for salvation on her and her God. Joe's refusal to submit himself to that formula threatens that myth for the sake of which she has continued to draw breath. She reacts to his recalcitrance, as the mob does later, by resorting to violence. Ironically the transformation of Joe Christmas into a Negro which she does not accomplish in her life is effected through her death.

Gail Hightower is, of course, rejected by Jefferson because he has proved himself unworthy of directing its religious, spiritual life. Like Joe Christmas and Joanna Burden, he is an impure element of which society must purge itself; and like them, he too mirrors yet another aspect of the South: its preoccupation with the legends of its own past. The exploits of the gallant Confederate forces are part of the inheritance of every Southern boy as well as an article in the belief of every Southern community. Such legends, provided they are accepted as legends, remain as valuable and harmless as the stories of Charlemagne. Hightower, however, sees a kind of revealed truth in the vision of his grandfather, compounded of an old Negress' storytelling and his own boyish imagination. The imagination is given full scope because there is nothing and no one to contradict his fictions. With an equal opportunity for deifying his father who also had a share in the glorious war, young Gail is unable to place the mantle of heroism on his shoulders. Thus, the dead grandfather becomes the symbol of "that fine shape of eternal youth and virginal desire which makes heroes," (423) while the living father evokes only the grim brutality and carnage of battle.

Eventually the legends of the past become the only truth and the only reality for Hightower, rendering his connection with the public world precarious at best. For unlike his father, he cannot function as "two separate and complete people, one of whom dwelled by serene rules in a world where reality did not exist." (415) And since nothing can compare with his vision, the people he meets and the tasks he is forced to perform become annoying interruptions of the commonplace and trivial. What destroys Hightower is not the fact that he has a dream, but that for the sake of the dream, he becomes insensitive and indifferent to the quality of his actual experience. Thus, he ignores his wife and her needs because the affection due her has already been pre-empted by her counterpart so that "when he did see her he did not see her at all because of the face which he had already created in his mind." (420) Dominated by his vision, he stands in the pulpit, fusing religion, the galloping cavalry, and his dead grandfather into one incoherent rhapsody, while he remains sublimely indifferent to the growing uneasiness of his parish and to the suicide of his wife.

As if recognizing that he has no place in Jefferson, that indeed his dream-world is threatened by it, Hightower deliberately provokes the violence which will ensure his isolation. For he can only justify and safeguard his withdrawal by "making it appear that he was being driven, uncomplaining, into that which he did not even then admit had been his desire since before he entered the seminary." (428) Each of his actions becomes a defiance, a calculated incentive to public outrage and retribution. Thus he, like Christmas, is at least partially responsible for his own isolation and for the violence he suffers. In his self-chosen role of antagonist, he experiences a fierce exultation, momentarily revealed by his demonic grin hidden by the prayer book. As passive victim, he suffers the threats and beating by the K.K.K. "with that patient and voluptuous ego of the martyr," (429) since it merely confirms his contemptuous judgment of society.

Safe at last in his lonely house, unvisited and undisturbed, Hightower yet retains one tenuous connection with the external world in the person of Byron Bunch. And it is Byron who ultimately forces him to re-examine his world and his life. Compelled by Byron to attend the birth of Lena's child, he becomes for the occasion a participant in rather than a spectator of life. But more important, through the birth he is initiated into the world of nature and discovers that life itself is a source of human value. Reversing his former opinion of Lena, he sees her as a symbol of life and a new paradise: *"That will be her life, her destiny. The good stock peopling in tranquil obedience to it the good earth."* (356)

Byron's plea that he at least attempt to save Joe Christmas is much more difficult to deal with. For though Hightower is willing to accept the natural world, he is not prepared to re-enter the social world. From the moment he hears of Christmas' Negro blood and of the murder, he knows beyond any doubt the sequence of events which must culminate in violence and death. He knows because he himself had been caught in a similar pattern. And though he feels pity, compassion even horror, he waits passively for the mob to turn once more "with insult and violence upon those who like them were created by the same God and were driven by them to do that which they now turn and rend them for having done it." (319–20) To interfere with the beliefs and rituals of society would be to admit his responsibility for that society. It would, in effect, expose the futility of a life devoted solely to the worship of a dream and to a world "intact and on all sides complete and inviolable, like a classic and serene vase, where the spirit could be born anew sheltered from the harsh gale of living." (419)

Nevertheless, when the escaped and fleeing Christmas rushes into his house, Hightower does make the one gesture which could give substance to his vision. Ironically, this one fumbling but heroic attempt to save Christmas at the risk of his own life, this one act which so far transcends practical considerations that it contains the germ of another legend, is nullified by a younger version of himself. Percy Grimm, engrossed in his own vision of military gallantary which has been fostered by a more recent war, sees nothing in Hightower's words but another example of the degrading crudeness of the non-military world. Too much has happened to Hightower and to Jefferson since the day he abandoned his chosen calling for him to be able to sway or influence the lynch-mob in any way. The past is irremediable.

Jarred out of his complacency and self-righteousness by Joe's death, Hightower sees his past with a new clarity. The image of the great wheel, which gives form to his memories, echoes and passes judgment on all the other solitary circles that have collided violently without ever establishing contact with one another. What he finally comes to recognize is the interdependence of the individual and society, of the private and public worlds, and, more important, the interdependence of individuals within the public world. He, Joe Christmas, and Joanna Burden have all been self-created martyrs to an idea and to that idea they have sacrificed others beyond themselves. Society, no less deluded, attacks and sacrifices them in the name of the same ideas. Their personal histories, like the history of Jefferson, consist of a perpetual denial of life for the sake of empty rituals, each of which enshrines some abstraction. Hightower has the intelligence to attain this bitter self-knowledge and to realize that the responsibility rests with the individual, but he does not have the strength to live with it. As his head falls to the window sill, he hears once again the thunderous cavalry charge peopling Jefferson with the old insubstantial phantoms.

Compared with the embattled lives and specter-haunted thoughts of Hightower, Christmas, and Miss Burden, the calm journey of Lena Grove with a willing Byron Bunch in her wake seems almost an impertinence. Yet it is through her presence that we achieve a final perspective on the action. Into the schematic world of Jefferson she introduces, by virtue of her own intellectual limitations and her pregnancy, the world of nature with its total indifference to both moral and social categories. This provides a significant contrast to Joe Christmas' painful initiation and absorption into society. Both are strangers to Jefferson; but while Joe comes bearing death for himself and others, Lena comes bearing life. The ritual in which she involves others is the natural one of pregnancy and birth. Thus, while the one crystallizes the obsessions of society, the other dispels them. The same almost anonymous figures who attach the label of Negro to Christmas in order to lynch him also forget the social stigma of Lena's pregnancy in order to help her.

Like Joe Christmas, Lena herself is a center for the actions and reactions of various characters and the object of a clearly defined public attitude. Each person she meets sees not her but an image of what he believes her to be, and that image is at least partly predetermined by the convention that identifies virginity with virtue. For Mrs. Armstid she is the fallen woman; for the men at the store, a foolish virgin to be treated with mingled pity and scorn; and for Byron, who loves her, she is the innocent victim of a scoundrel. Each of these images, grounded in a concern with Lena's unmarried state, conveys more information about the observers and their society than they do about her, for unlike Christmas, she does not mirror or share the preconceptions of the community. From the moment we see her delicately licking the sardine oil from her fingers, she is wholly absorbed in the new sensations with which her leisurely travels provide her. Even her search for a father for her child is more a matter of instinct than of morality. What she is looking for is security not respectability. Once Byron assumes this responsibility, she shows no great haste to marry and so to remove the social stigma from herself and her child.

Though Lena is judged harshly, she is consistently treated with kindness. The reason is that she offends against the mores of society without challenging its very foundations as Joe Christmas does. In a sense, the community's convictions and actions operate independently. Mrs. Armstid or the men who offer Lena a ride preserve the myth of virginity in which they share by revealing their contempt for the unmarried Lena, but at the same time they respond to her needs as a woman about to give birth to a child. Here the pressing demands of nature take precedence over social convention.

Thus Lena's arrival signals the breaking up of the old compulsive patterns which match action to judgment. Mrs. Armstid's tight-lipped offer of food, shelter, and money prepares us for Byron's quick abandonment of his routine of overtime work and weekly trips to the country church when Lena appears. He too acts "contrary to all the tradition of his austere and jealous country raising which demands in the object physical inviolability." (42) It is not, however, until Mrs. Hines calls him to the cabin where Lena is in labor that he fully realizes and admits to himself that she is not a virgin. Hightower, despite his distrust of Lena and his fear of Byron, disrupts the pattern of his life and leaves his sanctuary to attend the birth of her child. The sheriff, momentarily overlooking the letter of the law, recognizes her need and therefore her right to use Miss Burden's cottage. Even the anonymous truck driver is trapped into kindness towards Lena and gives up his bed, though not the right to grumble about it.

In each of these cases, the separation of judgment and action is made possible by Lena's own indifference to the former. The relationship between society and the individual is reciprocal as the lives of Hightower, Miss Burden, and Christmas amply illustrate. But Lena refuses or rather is incapable of acting in the light of society's preconception of her. Accordingly, where Joe Christmas intensifies, she destroys the barriers between herself and others; where he forever threatens life with extinction, she becomes the means of its renewal and continuance. This difference is made explicit by the incidents involving food. Lena herself is indifferent to the spirit in which it is offered so long as it sustains her and her child. And her acceptance of it invariably fosters a more personal, human relationship with the giver. Christmas, on the other hand, is forever rejecting the food offered him because of his abnormal sensitivity to the thoughts and attitudes of the giver. He is able to share food with Bobbie, believing that she loves him, but he consistently rejects meals offered by Mrs. McEachern, Byron Bunch, or Miss Burden. The food which sustains Lena in her world of physical experience proves poisonous to Christmas, who lives largely in a world of obsessive ideas which he projects, rightly or wrongly, into every situation. Joe and Lena thus present two contrasting attitudes to experience and to society, and these in turn evoke sharply different responses from society.

Both make a claim on Byron Bunch, the one uncommitted character in the novel, since he has isolated himself from both nature and society. But it is his love for Lena and his sudden and unexpected initiation into the world of nature which she represents that makes Byron willing and eager to help Christmas. Her needs destroy those protective barriers of meaningless routine which he has built around himself. As Hightower points out, Byron, by loving her, becomes vulnerable, for he has allowed himself to be caught up in a chain of events and circumstances over which he can exercise no control. At the same time, however, he has gained in some measure a self-respect, a dignity, and a courage which was lacking in his isolated safety and which gives promise of being a sufficient shield against whatever catastrophes he may encounter. His romantic desire to protect Lena, to convert Hightower, and to save Christmas appear, at first sight, exaggerated reactions to his former passivity and belief in non-interference. But the important thing is that he does not rest in these attitudes or treat his vision of Lena as immutable. He is still necessarily the creator of his own world, but now he is willing to recognize when he has built awry and to reshape it with an eye to reality.

His ability to do so is dependent, to a large extent, on his eventual discovery of the resources of humor. His love for Lena, itself an irrational act, makes him realize the comic aspect of his own behavior. By laughing at his own follies and gullibility, he is able to continue acting irrationally which, in this case, is also humanely; for laughter is one means of re-examining the shibboleths of society and of placing the individual and his world once more in perspective. Though Byron is still sustained by illusions, he is no longer blindly ruled by them. Instead he endeavors through them to establish his kinship with other men. Though he continues to believe in Lena's chastity, Hightower's wisdom, and Joe's black blood, nevertheless, he arranges for the confinement, argues for the first time with Hightower, and does what little he can to help Joe. His illusions are thus more nearly centered on humanity and grounded in the immediacy of living experience. It is man's nature to dream and dreams by their very essence are both distortions of reality and desires for a new shape to experience.

Certainly, the real Lena, more than slightly stupid and more than slightly selfish, and the real Confederate Hightower, who found an inglorious death in a chickencoop, are both unworthy of the dreams and the devotion they inspire. The responsibility, however, lies not with them but with the Byron Bunches and Gail Hightowers who can be moved to save or to deny Joe Christmas because of their dreams. Reason and imagination can prove an integrative force, identifying the interest of the individual with those of the community and establishing a link between the private and public worlds. They can also be destructive insofar as they enable man to invent infinitely various excuses which permit him to live while ignoring life itself. Rationally conceived categories and myths may render morality simpler and clearer by providing formulas of universal applicability, but in the process they destroy those essential motives for morality which must be found by the individual in life itself. This is the truth that Hightower could only know; it is also the truth which Byron, in fumbling and often farcically inadequate fashion, seeks to live.

Frozen Movement in *Light in August*

by Darrel Abel

I. Symbol

Faulkner's *Light in August* does not (except within the arbitrary perspective of any given character in the novel) delineate a single complete action with a beginning, a middle, and an end. For Faulkner's reality, like Bergson's, is a "becomingness"—not static, but dynamic; not formed, but fluid. To Faulkner, "The present does not exist, it becomes. . . ." [1] According to Bergson, "Reality is mobility. There do not exist *things* made, but only things in the making, not *states* that remain fixed, but only states in process of change." [2]

A writer . . . escape[s] from the static and particular into the vital and general . . . [through] the poetic faculty alluded to in "Tintern Abbey," by which "the heavy and the weary weight / Of all this unintelligible world is lightened" and "We see into the life of things." . . . [In short, the poet's] technique must master a paradox: in order to fix reality in a literary construct, it must freeze movement. "Faulkner appears to arrest the motion at the very heart of things; moments

---

"Frozen Movement in Light in August*" by Darrel Abel. From* Boston University Studies in English, *III (1957), 32–44. Condensed and reprinted with the permission of the author and the publisher.*

[1] Jean-Paul Sartre, "Time in Faulkner: *The Sound and the Fury*," trans. Martine Darmon, in Frederick J. Hoffman and Olga W. Vickery, *William Faulkner: Two Decades of Criticism* (East Lansing, Michigan: Michigan State College Press, 1954), p. 183. Reprinted from *Situations*, I, "Le Bruit et la fureur" (Paris: Gallimard, 1947), pp. 70–81.

[2] Quoted by permission of the publishers, The Philosophical Library, from Henri Bergson, *The Creative Mind*, trans. Mabelle L. Andison (New York: The Philosophical Library, 1946), p. 222. All subsequent quotations cited by page numbers enclosed in parentheses in the text refer to this edition.

erupt and freeze, then fade, recede and diminish, still motionless." [3] . . .

In *Light in August* Faulkner attempts to contrive through symbols an immobile representation of mobility, and at the same time to suggest how "relative" and arbitrary any distinct and arranged version of mobile reality must be. He endeavors to represent a fluid reality in the static terms "necessary to common sense, to language, to practical life"; and at the same time to disclose that the static images through which he makes the fluid reality visible are merely arrested and discontinuous blinks—what Bergson calls "snapshots" or "cuttings made out of the becoming" (pp. 227, 222, 39).

Such a symbolic shuttering of reality controls the narration from the opening pages, which offer an image, immediately augmented into a symbol,[4] of the mule-drawn country wagons in which Lena Grove made her enchanted, ineluctable progress from Alabama into Mississippi; "back-rolling now behind her a long monotonous succession of peaceful and undeviating changes from day to dark and dark to day again, through which she advances in identical and monotonous and deliberate wagons as though through a succession of creak-wheeled and limp-eared avatars, like something moving forever and without progress across an urn." [5]

In this figure the countryside across which Lena travels is, like the "silent form" of Keats's urn,[6] a designated image or visible metaphor of eternity. The stories of Lena Grove and Joe Christmas constitute the "legend" (or "brede" or "frieze") seen against this immutable image of eternity. A legend is both an inscription and an old story, especially an "old story" in the colloquial sense of something happening over and

[3] Sartre, "Time in Faulkner," p. 182.

[4] I use the terms "image," "symbol," and "figure" in this paper in the different senses which I think they usually carry: "image"—a distinct, unified sense-impression of an object; "symbol"—an image which is the nucleus and sign of a congeries of not readily explicable meanings and sensations; "figure"—pattern or design, possibly a configuration of images in time or space; also, any kind of trope.

[5] Quoted by permission of the publishers, Random House, from William Faulkner, *Light in August* (New York: Modern Library, 1950), Chap. I. All subsequent quotations cited by chapter numbers enclosed in parentheses in the text refer to this book.

[6] For more explicit allusions by Faulkner to Keats's "Ode to a Grecian Urn" which show how persistently Keats's urn-symbol has haunted Faulkner's imagination, see Faulkner's article "Verse Old and Nascant: A Pilgrimage," *Double-Dealer,* VII (1925), 130; and "The Bear," *Go Down, Moses* (New York: Modern Library, 1955), p. 297. Norman Holmes Pearson has commented on Keats's urn-symbol as employed in *Light in August* in "Lena Grove," *Shenandoah,* III (1951), 3–7.

over again from time immemorial. Against the background of country-side which is Faulkner's equivalent of the "silent form" of Keats's urn, the comic and pathetic leaf-fring'd [7] legends of Lena Grove and Joe Christmas are seen to be, although interesting as individual histories, even more significant as expressions, moments, postures, phases of a human reality into which all personal realities fade. The stillness of urn and countryside represent, not immobility itself, but "deserts of vast eternity"—so vast that in such perspective all particulars and moments are lost.

Faulkner's somewhat peculiar use of the word "avatar," in characterizing the progressive appearances or apparent progress of both Lena Grove and Joe Christmas through space and time, makes their stories legends of arrested human striving like the "brede / Of marble men and maidens" on the urn. Lena "advances as though through a succession of avatars"; Joe, "as in numberless avatars" (Chaps. I, X). The main signification in Faulkner's use of the term "avatar" is of course simply "embodiment." [8] The avatar-figure, which converts personal histories into a mere succession of envisagements of a continuous and moving process of human "becoming," determines the conception of the other characters in the novel too. In Faulkner's sense of "avatar," Hightower's whole inert existence is a kind of prolonged or aborted avatar, in consequence of his belief "that I skipped a generation. . . .

---

[7] Professor Pearson ("Lena Grove," p. 6) remarks that Lena's family name (Grove) alludes to the "leaf-fring'd"; probably, despite the change of vowel, Burch's name also has this reference. That *Light in August* is "a kind of pastoral" has been noted by Cleanth Brooks in "Notes on Faulkner's 'Light in August,'" *Harvard Advocate*, CXXXV (1951), 27.

[8] Thus, for example, Faulkner calls the old mulatto Lucas Beauchamp in *Intruder in the Dust* an "avatar" ("Lucas in ten thousand Sambo-avatars") of the Negro in a position of moral superiority to the white man who has injured him (*Intruder in the Dust* [New York: New American Library, "Signet Books"], Chap. IX). In the "Appendix" to *The Sound and the Fury* which he wrote for *The Portable Faulkner*, ed. Malcolm Cowley (New York: Viking Press, 1946), Faulkner speaks of old Brigadier General Jason Lycurgus Compson II as "now completing the third of his three avatars—the one as son of a brilliant and gallant statesman, the second as battle-leader of brave and gallant men, the third as a sort of privileged pseudo-Daniel Boone-Robinson Crusoe." In the same "Appendix" Faulkner tells of Jefferson's mousy librarian spending "her life trying to keep *Forever Amber* in its orderly overlapping avatars . . . out of the hands of highschool juniors and seniors": the "avatars" of *Forever Amber,* that is, are the whole succession of forbidden sexy novels which titillate feverish adolescent fancy. "Avatar," in these various instances, seems to signify a periodic succession of embodiments of an essentially identical reality—or, as in "ten thousand Sambo-avatars," perhaps multiple simultaneous embodiments.

I had already died one night twenty years before I saw light" (Chap. XX). Even Byron Bunch philosophically questions his own determinateness as a self, his own identity: *"You just say that you are Byron Bunch. . . . You are just the one that calls yourself Byron Bunch today, now, this minute"* (Chap. XVIII). Faulkner apparently uses the avatar-figure to indicate that a person's sense of distinct and stable identity is simply a hypostatization of the streaming subjective life in which he transiently exists and which his private consciousness defines for him as *his* life.

A less conspicuous device of Faulkner's for indicating that the "fixed" is only an arbitrary arrest of the "moving" is his frequent mention of the omnipresent muted hum of natural life,[9] furnishing a vague, monotonous, repetitive, generalized accompaniment to foreground action. Thus Joe Christmas, voicing his finally definite intention to murder Joanna Burden, heard around him "a myriad sounds, . . . voices, murmurs, whispers: of trees, darkness, earth, people: his own voice; other voices evocative of names and times and places . . ." (Chap. V). As he entered the house later, to commit the deed, "The dark was filled with voices, myriad, out of all time that he had known, as though all the past was a flat pattern. And going on: tomorrow night, all the tomorrows, to be a part of the flat pattern, going on" (Chap. XII). After Christmas' capture, as Hightower hears from Mrs. Hines the story of his early life, "through the open window there comes now only the peaceful and myriad sounds of the summer night" (Chap. XVI). And later, as Hightower is alone in his house, struggling to suppress his humane impulse to sympathize with and help "poor mankind": "Beyond the open window the sound of insects has not ceased, has not faltered" (Chap. XVI). These generalized, remote, anonymous voices of changing, enduring reality constitute an audible image of the continuous and moving, just as urn and countryside are its visible image.

If, then, *Light in August* eschews classical form—lacks a single complete action with a beginning, a middle, and an end—it does so because there is no alpha or omega in Faulkner's alphabet of reality. His novel ends, but his story does not: it is merely a harsh and prolonged suspiration swelling out of and subsiding into the "myriad voices, out of all time." Faulkner's story is about convergent or con-

---

[9] Faulkner's "myriad voices, out of all time" correspond to what Bergson calls "the uninterrupted humming of life's depths" (pp. 176–177). Faulkner externalizes and objectifies the concept by finding an "objective correlative": the summertime chorus of insect-sounds.

nected human destinies, which have as their nexus the burning of the Burden house, an event which any individual character views as a fixed and understood reality, but which is in fact a symbol capable of as many significances as the various individuals who view it are enabled to read into it from their own experience, their own ideas. To the stranger who brings Lena to Jefferson, it is merely "a house burning" (Chap. I). But as a crucial moment in each of the human histories which converge in it, it is variously interpreted. To each, it brings "light in August" in a different way, provides a glaring but transient interval of illumination and realization.

II. Story

"There is at least one reality which we all seize from within, by intuition and not by simple analysis. It is our own person in its flowing through time, the self which endures" (p. 191). "If, instead of claiming to analyze duration . . . , one first installs oneself in it by an effort of intuition, one has the feeling of a certain well-defined *tension,* whose very definiteness seems like a choice between an infinity of possible durations" (p. 218). The central perception offered to readers of *Light in August* is expressed in Bergson's sentence, "The higher the consciousness, the stronger is this tension of its own duration in relation to that of things" (p. 105). Such a "tension" requires a consciousness of at least two "possible durations": the intuition of our own duration, "which we all seize from within"; and the intuition of some possible duration more comprehensive than our own. Duration consists of "the addition to the present feeling, of the memory of past moments" (p. 211). "The distinction between our present and past is . . . , if not arbitrary, at least relative to the extent of the field which our attention to life can embrace" (p. 179). Thus, intuitions grasp "durations" which vary infinitely in comprehensiveness. They may include awareness of immediate and instant reality, or of our whole lives since birth, or of generations of our family, or of the continuing life of the human species, or of the vast transcendent flux in which the *élan vital* endlessly reshapes reality in novel and more complex forms.

Of the major characters in *Light in August,* the one with least awareness of "this tension of its own duration in relation to that of things" is Lena Grove, for her intuition of her own duration is a very contracted one, and she has no intuition of any other duration. Her "attention to life" embraces only what immediately confronts her; there is little addition to her present feeling "of memory of past events." She cares nothing for her own past or for her family, and never thinks of them; she is fully content with the moment which she occupies, and with the bliss of being in it. As the book opens, she reflects, *"Although I have not been quite a month on the road I am already in Mississippi";* and as it ends, she says, "Here we aint been coming from Alabama but two months, and now it's already Tennessee" (Chaps. I, XXI). The brief span of her attention to the past is clearly marked in such reflections: the only past she ever speaks of is a very recent one, and she speaks of it only as the antecedent of the present in which she is almost wholly engrossed. Her consciousness has "an inward-lighted quality of tranquil and calm unreason" (Chap. I). "The duration of things" is not measured for her by the tides of God or the clocks and calendars of man, but solely by the elemental urges and responses of her nature to her immediate surroundings. She knows no reality beyond her subjective moment. She represents ordinary naive mankind, inviolably innocent because it cannot enter the realm of ideas. To Hightower she stands for *"the good stock peopling in tranquil obedience to it the good earth"* (Chap. XVII). She is too unsophisticated to comprehend good and evil. Faulkner assigns her the first and last speeches of the novel because, just as hers is the least conscious and sophisticated, so is it the most elemental and enduring, aspect of humanity. She is one of Sandburg's "people who live on," a primitive character like Hardy's "man harrowing clods."

If *Light in August* at all anticipates Faulkner's later statement, in his Nobel Prize acceptance speech, that "man will not merely endure; he will prevail," it does so by identifying the "crucified" Joe Christmas with Lena's child, and by exhibiting her calm and confident onward travel at the end of the story. The hate, mistrust, and evil will which impel mankind to crucify some of its members are counterbalanced by the love, trust, and good will tendered to Lena and her child. Lena prevails, not by her understanding, but by her complacent trust in others, a trust amounting almost to obstinacy and stupidity. Although her story is a comedy of rustic innocence, a comic pastoral, Faulkner dignifies instead of disparaging her.

In contrast, Joe Christmas' story is tragic, or at least pathetic. Although Lena is hardly more than an expression of the will to live of the species, Joe is a person struggling to establish his selfhood, and aware of overwhelming influences extending into his life from a long reach of time and a broad range of human relationships. He saw his own history as a struggle to gain status in white society, or, failing that, to revert to primitivism. A long passage near the end of Chapter V serves as figure for his life. It relates how, on the night before he murdered Joanna Burden, he wandered into the Negro section of Jefferson, Freedman Town, "like a phantom, a spirit, strayed out of its own world and lost. . . . It was as though he and all other manshaped life about him had been returned to the lightless hot wet primogenitive Female." He ran in frantic revulsion "out of the black hollow," but became calm when he reached a white neighborhood with "clustered lights: low bright birds in stillwinged and tremulous suspension." He said of the white life around him, "That's all I wanted. . . . That dont seem a whole lot to ask." As he walked on, he saw behind him "the far bright rampart of the town . . . and the black pit from which he had fled . . . black, impenetrable, in its garland of August-tremulous lights. It might have been the original quarry, abyss itself" (Chap. V).

In retrospect Christmas saw his career as a vain striving to emerge from the black, primitive, earthly, female, passionate "allmother of obscurity and darkness" (Chap. X) into light, civilization, manliness, volition, identity. In the course of this vain striving, his hatred of the "lightless hot wet primogenitive Female" grew into a complex obsession. His first indelible impressions, at the orphanage, were of females, sex, guilt, and the rejection of Negroes as inflictions divinely and irrevocably decreed. At the McEacherns', throughout his boyhood, these impressions were all confirmed and deepened. His first experience of sex made it for him thereafter simply an overmastering lust: "something liquid, deathcolored and foul" (Chap. VIII). After his young innocence and affection had been outraged by the malformed whore Bobbie Allen (an episode grotesquely caricaturing love's young dream), he tried to coerce by injury and hate the world into which he could not find a way by generosity and love. Even at the age of five in the orphanage he had learned to believe that *"I am different from the others"* (Chap. VI), and he never was able to surmount the difference.

After his decisive rejection by the white world, he tried to return to primitive black life. In Detroit

he lived with Negroes, shunning white people. . . . He now lived as man and wife with a woman who resembled an ebony carving. At night he would lie in bed beside her, . . . trying to breathe into himself the dark odor, the dark and inscrutable thinking and being of Negroes, with each suspiration trying to expel from himself the white blood and the white thinking and being. And all the while his nostrils at the odor which he was trying to make his own would whiten and tauten, his whole being writhe and strain with physical outrage and spiritual denial. (Chap. X)

Christmas failed to recover "the dark and inscrutable thinking and being of Negroes," not because they refused to accept him, but because his upbringing had conditioned him against it. He had not gained a place in the white world, but he had been unfitted for a place in the black world. His was the tragedy of "black blood" in a "pale body" (Chap. XIX), an antagonism of two possibilities so equal in strength that each negated the other. Thus Gavin Stevens summed up his tragedy:

> It was not alone all those thirty years [of his personal existence] . . . , but all those successions of thirty years before that which had put that stain either on his white blood or his black blood, whichever you will, and which killed him. . . . His blood would not be quiet. . . . It would not be either one or the other. (Chap. XIX)

Thus Faulkner shows that the conviction of his outcast fate which dogged "Christmas, the son of Joe" (Chap. XVI) grew in his mind like a fatality. When he anticipated murdering Joanna Burden, he did not acknowledge that he willed to do it, but that he was fated to do it: *"Something is going to happen to me"* (Chap. V). When he murdered her, he "believed with calm paradox that he was the volitionless servant of the fatality[10] in which he believed that he did not believe" (Chap. XII). He transvaluated murder into something like a creative act, however, since it was for him a symbolic annihilation of the world which had denied his claims to selfhood and status. Joanna Burden was his appropriate victim, for she combined in one person the three elements of coercion which Joe had experienced: femaleness, Calvinism, and obsession with color-difference.[11]

Since Christmas could not find a secure life anywhere, his only al-

[10] Most of the principal characters in the novel (Grimm, McEachern, Joanna Burden, and even Gail Hightower) act as if their wills were determined by some overruling necessity. For an excellent brief discussion of the theme of fatality in Faulkner, see Rabi, "Faulkner and the Exiled Generation," in *William Faulkner: Two Decades of Criticism*, especially pp. 132–134.

[11] For discussion of the conjoined Negro-sex motifs in *Light in August* see Phyllis Hirshleifer, "As Whirlwinds in the South: An Analysis of *Light in August*," *Perspective*, II (1949), 237–238.

ternative was to die: to accept and hasten the doom that he thought was determined for him. After the murder, as he looked at his feet in the black Negro shoes that he had put on to throw the pursuing bloodhounds off the scent, it "seemed to him that he could see himself being hunted by white men at last into the black abyss, which had been waiting, trying, for thirty years to drown him and into which now and at last he had actually entered, bearing upon his ankles the definite and ineradicable gauge of its upward moving" (Chap. XIV).

Just as Lena represents the comedy of ordinary life, so does Joe represent the tragedy of extraordinary life. Hated, corrupted, and persecuted from the hour of his birth, he was not only accused of being evil by those who "crucified" him for righteousness' sake (Hines in the name of God, Grimm in the name of patriotism and society); he *was* evil, for he had been imbued with all the sin and corruption of humanity; he was a scapegoat burdened with the accumulated evils of his generation. But even his persecutors were not responsible for the tragedy. Although Hines and Grimm were persecutors rather than victims, although Lucas Burch was Judas rather than Christ, all alike were servants of the general and traditional obsessions which assigned their roles in the tragedy. Byron Bunch's opinion about the town of Jefferson's long harassment of Hightower applies equally well to Christmas' "crucifixion": "The entire affair had been a lot of people performing a play and . . . now and at last they had all played out the parts that had been allotted to them" (Chap. III).

III. Coda

"Installed in universal mobility, . . . consciousness contracts in a quasi-instantaneous vision an immensely long history which unfolds outside it. The higher the consciousness, the stronger is this tension of its own duration in relation to that of things" (p. 105). Gail Hightower is the most significant character in *Light in August* because only he attained the higher consciousness which "contracts in a quasi-instantaneous vision an immensely long history which unfolds outside it." Hightower suffered even more than Joe Christmas, for he who experiences most suffers most. Hightower tried to maintain that he had "bought immunity" (Chap. XIII) from involvement in the affairs of living men, but his long-suppressed humanity impelled him "to come back into life" (Chap. XIII) to assist at a birth and try to prevent a death. His identification with the human beings whose fates, when he was forced to sympathize with them, illustrated both the hopeful and tragic possibilities of the life he had evaded, made him comprehend the general fate of mankind, which is to serve the compulsive ideas which are its inheritance. Hightower's own story is an exaggerated rendering of the truth that all men are directed by ancestral ghosts and do not fully possess their own realities. He had chosen to withdraw into his ancestral ghost, rather than to let the human past summed up in him enter the present; but his story, like Joanna Burden's and Joe Christmas', shows the persistence through generations of a pattern of transmitted ideas and tendencies which effectually make each inheritor their instrument, because they are not externally dictated to him but are constitutive of his own character.

Because Hightower had so long lived a "dead life in the actual world," "dissociated from mechanical time" (Chap. XVI), had not enacted a vital role in the present, he was able, like God in a high tower in a medieval mystery play, to see that present with detachment. He had breadth of understanding and depth of compassion, and rose to contemplation of those principles of human action, those conditions of human life, which are so recurrent in time that they seem ulterior to time, and "tease us out of thought/As doth eternity." . . . Lena Grove, a pagan generatrix, is mankind aware of its existence only through participation in the burgeoning life of nature; Joe Christmas lives and dies in a world of ideas of good and evil; but Gail Hightower, by his intuition of "universal mobility," philosophically transcends both the natural and moral worlds.

The concluding revery of Hightower (to whom light in August comes more effulgently than to any other character, although all the witnesses of Christmas' death . . . have a half-comprehended enlightenment) shows him in an instant when "consciousness contracts in a quasi-instantaneous vision an immensely long history which unfolds outside itself." In his agony of comprehension, of realization, Hightower sits "in the lambent suspension of August into which night is about fully to come," and all the faces of the recent past rise before him, but "not shaped with suffering, not shaped with anything: not horror, pain, not even reproach. They are peaceful, as though they have escaped into an apotheosis" (Chap. XX). The figure which structures his revery is a rapidly revolving wheel of thought,[12] or consciousness, which slows

[12] Faulkner, in representing what Bergson calls "intuition of duration," generally uses cyclic figures. Movement across an urn is of course cyclic movement. Joe Christmas feels that for thirty years he has been running "inside a circle" (Chap. XIV). Lena thinks of her movement along a country road as being "like measured

and stops to focus the static images and characters which perception distinguishes in the continuous, moving reality. But the wheel in rapid revolution is a halo full of faces that "all look alike, composite of all the faces that he has ever seen" (Chap. XX).

In this apocalyptic instant in Hightower's vision the faces of Christmas and Grimm, in mortal life obsessed and murderous opponents, "fade and blend." "Then it seems to [Hightower] that some ultimate dammed flood within him breaks and rushes away. He seems to watch it, feeling himself losing contact with earth, lighter and lighter, emptying, floating. . . . [He thinks,] 'With all air, all heaven, filled with the lost and unheeded crying of all the living who ever lived, wailing still like lost children among the cold and terrible stars. . . .'" (Chap. XX). Thus, for an instant, Hightower escapes from the static and discontinuous appearances which constitute reality to ordinary perception: leaves the temporal world of frieze and legend and enters the eternity of the urn-world itself. When, by philosophic intuition, man is able to "arise from a frozen vision of the real . . . to perceive all things *sub specie durationis*," "all things acquire depth,—more than depth, something like a fourth dimension. . . . What was immobile and frozen in our perception is warmed and set in motion. Everything comes to life around us. . . . A great impulse carries beings and things along. We feel ourselves uplifted, carried away, borne along by it" (p. 186). In the Dionysian dance of life there comes a serene moment of Apollonian vision.

The climactic symbol of *Light in August,* the lambent wheel which Hightower sees in his highest moment of vision as an image of eternity, is an archetypal symbol whose richness can be best apprehended in comparison with literary parallels. The most obvious is Dante's recurrent conjunction of images of light and a rapidly revolving wheel in the *Paradiso* (e.g., Cantos, i, xii, xxviii), especially the elaborate image of the circle of fire, or rapidly whirling wheel haloed with

---

thread being rewound onto a spool" (Chap. I). This simile is also used by Bergson to suggest the sense of "our own person in its flowing through time" (p. 191): "It is, if you like, like the unrolling of a spool. . . . But it is just as much a continual winding, like that of thread into a ball" (pp. 192–193). Richard Chase has discussed the contrasting significances of what he calls "linear discreteness and curve" in "The Stone and the Crucifixion: Faulkner's *Light in August*," *Kenyon Review,* X (1948), 539–551 (reprinted in *William Faulkner: Two Decades of Criticism*). I think that his argument, although perceptive and valuable, miscarries somewhat because he thinks in terms of the form of Faulkner's cyclic images, instead of noting that they are essentially images of duration.

light, which Dante views in the ninth heaven (Canto xxviii). Dante quotes in connection with this image a passage from Aristotle's *Metaphysics* on the *primum mobile,* the "unmoved mover" which is the center and source of this dazzle of cyclic movement. Similarly, Plato's *Timaeus* designates the stars in their courses as "a moving image of eternity"—a passage which may be the source of the famous opening stanza of Henry Vaughan's poem "The World":

> I saw Eternity the other night
> Like a great ring of pure and endless light,
> All calm, as it was bright,
> And round beneath it, Time, in hours, days, years,
> Driven by the spheres
> Like a vast shadow moved, in which the world
> And all her train were hurl'd.

I think it likely that such reminiscences, whether conscious or not, have contributed to Faulkner's symbol of the haloed wheel of Hightower's vision. If Hightower, like Dante, is regarded as one who, while still in mortal life, is afforded a vision of eternity in all its phases, his experience exhibits something of hell, of purgatory, and of heaven. His inferno consists of his witnessing and participating in the complicated tragedy of human evil and mortality which is consummated in the "crucifixion" of Joe Christmas. His purgatory is the initial stage of his revery after Christmas' death, when finally, in "a consternation which is about to be actual horror," he admits his guilt as an "instrument of [his wife's] despair and shame," while "sweat begins to pour from him, springing out like blood" (Chap. XX). He sees, beyond his own guilt, the determinism which fixed this complicity in evil upon him: "If I am the instrument of her despair and death, then I am in turn instrument of someone outside myself" (Chap. XX). Purged by his abandonment of delusion, his admission of truth, he enters his paradise, his moment of perception of an eternal truth which leaves his stale and corrupt "body empty and lighter than a forgotten leaf and even more trivial than flotsam lying spent and still . . . ; so that it can be now Now" [13] (Chap. XX).

But, although *Light in August* contains a *Divina commedia,* a *Comédie humaine* encompasses it: Lena, the almost primitive embodi-

[13] Faulkner's "now Now" is a verbal device for signaling the moment of Hightower's passage from a temporal now to the Eternal Now. Compare "yesterday today and tomorrow are Is: Indivisible: One" (*Intruder in the Dust,* Chap. IX).

ment of the human species' persistent effort to seek attachments and find durable satisfactions in local, temporal, and personal terms, is presented to us first and last. Her primacy in the story does not mean, I think, that Faulkner rejects Hightower's vision of reality for her view of it, but rather that he regards Lena's reality as the almost universally and constantly available one, and Hightower's as a difficult, fleeting, and rarely attainable one.

The Community and the Pariah

by Cleanth Brooks

. . . [N]early all the characters in [*Light in August*] are drawn from the ranks of the plain people and most of them exhibit a Puritan ethic. They are in tension with nature, and some have even been deformed and perverted in a struggle against it. The theme of man strained away from nature, however, is only one of several significant Faulknerian themes to be found in *Light in August*. . . . The community . . . is the powerful though invisible force that quietly exerts itself in so much of Faulkner's work. It is the circumambient atmosphere, the essential ether of Faulkner's fiction. But for many a reader, the community is indeed invisible and quite imperceptible: it exerts no pressure on him at all—and lacking any awareness of this force, he may miss the meaning of the work. Such readers find *Light in August* quite baffling simply because they are unaware of the force of community that pervades it and thus miss the clue to its central structure.

Yet a little reflection will show that nearly all the characters in *Light in August* bear a special relation to the community. They are outcasts—they are pariahs, defiant exiles, withdrawn quietists, or simply strangers. Miss Burden, the daughter of carpetbagger intruders, has lived for years within what can be described only as a kind of cultural cyst. The community has tried its best to expel the Reverend Mr. Hightower, though having failed in the attempt it has finally accorded him a sort of grudging acceptance. Joe Christmas is, of course, Ishmael himself, actively defying the community. Even Byron Bunch fits into this pattern of alienation. Byron, with his methodical earnestness and his countrified asceticism, is regarded as a kind of eccentric—a "charac-

"The Community and the Pariah." From William Faulkner: The Yoknapatawpha Country *by Cleanth Brooks (New Haven and London: Yale University Press, 1963), pp. 47–74. Copyright © 1963 by Yale University. Condensed and reprinted with the permission of the publisher.*

ter." For "seven years [he] had been a minor mystery to the town" (p. 369).

But the community itself, the great counterforce to which these characters are attracted or against which they are reacting, has no special representatives in the novel and need have none. For the community, everywhere in the novel, is visible to the reader who is prepared to see it. It expresses itself through Mrs. Armstid emptying her china bank and knotting the coins into a sack for Lena; through the sheriff kicking the ineffectual bloodhounds or ordering the thrill-seekers away from his examination of the Negro witness; through the second-hand furniture dealer who relates the closing episode of the novel; and through a dozen other minor or anonymous characters.

Sometimes the author makes an explicit comment upon the community, as he does in the long and brilliantly handled account of Gail Hightower in Chapter 3. After Mrs. Hightower's shameful death, the community is sure that Hightower will resign his church. When he does so at last, after persistent moral pressure, the town is glad. "Then the town was sorry with being glad, as people sometimes are sorry for those whom they have at last forced to do as they wanted them to" (p. 60). But Hightower still would not leave the town, and the community was furious with him for his stubbornness. Finally, some men took him out and beat him, and the townspeople, now horrified, offered "to prosecute the men who had done it" (p. 62). But Hightower refused to tell who his assailants were. "Then all of a sudden the whole thing seemed to blow away, like an evil wind. It was as though the town realized at last that he would be a part of its life until he died, and that they might as well become reconciled." Neighbors once more began to leave baskets of food upon his porch— "though they were the sort of dishes which they would have sent to a poor mill family. But it was food, and wellmeant" (p. 63).

. . . The plight of the isolated individual cut off from any community of values is of course a dominant theme of contemporary literature. But by developing this theme in a rural setting in which a powerful sense of community still exists, Faulkner has given us a kind of pastoral—that is, he has let us see our modern and complex problems mirrored in a simpler and more primitive world. *Light in August* is, in some respects, a bloody and violent pastoral. The plight of the lost sheep and of the black sheep can be given special point and meaning because there is still visible in the background a recognizable flock with its shepherds, its watchdogs, sometimes fierce and cruel, and its bellwethers.

Yet the reader of *Light in August* may still question the relation of the fact of community to the meaning of the novel. Granted that the community is a living force, what does that have to do with the meaning of the novel? And he can scarcely be blamed if he goes on to ask whether *Light in August* is a novel at all. What possible relation is there between the two main characters, Lena and Joe Christmas, who never meet and who go their separate ways, the one placidly, the other violently? There is obviously the bare fact of contrast; but is there anything more? Do not these characters between them rend the book in two? [1]

Both questions are in order. A proper answer to the first (the relation of the community to the meaning of this novel) will suggest an answer to the second (the unity of the novel). But the answer to the first cannot be succinct, and in any case we must begin by considering more fully the relations of the various characters—to each other and to the world around them.

Lena and Joe Christmas, as everyone has seen, stand in obvious contrast to each other. Their very likenesses stress their basic differences. Both are orphans; both escape from home by crawling out a window; both are betrayed by their first loves; both in the course of their wanderings come to Jefferson. But how different they are in relation to society! Every man's hand is sooner or later lifted against Joe Christmas; he demands that it be so. But Lena, heavy with child, on an obviously ridiculous quest to find the father of her child, leads a charmed life. Even the women who look upon her swollen body with evident disapproval press their small store of coins upon her, and the community in general rallies to help her. As Mrs. Beard remarks to Byron Bunch: "Aint you and that preacher and ever other man that knows about her already done everything for her that she could think to want?" (p. 368). In the person of Bunch, her quixotic errand actually raises up for her an authentic though clumsy knight-errant, who becomes her protector and fights her battles.

Joe repels, Lena attracts the force of the community into which they both come as strangers. But the point is not that Lena is "good" and Joe "bad." Joe's alienation from the community is not simply "willed" —there are deep-seated reasons for it, and, moreover, his is only the most extreme of a whole series of such alienations.

Faulkner has documented each history of alienation rather carefully,

[1] See, for example, Richard Rovere's introduction to the [1950] Modern Library edition.

and has done so in great detail with those of Joe Christmas and Gail
Hightower. Hightower, because of certain warping influences in childhood, becomes fettered to the past. Because of certain traumatic experiences in childhood, Christmas is cut off from any meaningful past.
Hightower toward the end of the novel comes to the bitter realization
that he has hardly lived at all. The son of middle-aged parents (his
father fifty, his mother forty), brought up in an austere house, he came
as a child to dote upon the memory of his Confederate cavalryman
grandfather, who represented all that his father was not. Hightower
regards his father as an enemy. As he puts it, "I skipped a generation"
(p. 418). He is able to invest his grandfather's death (he was shot
while robbing a henhouse on some foraging expedition) with romantic
glamour. His sermons mix up in an incredible farrago the charging
cavalry with the word of God. Late in the novel he comes to admit to
himself that "for fifty years" he has "not even been clay: I have been a
single instant of darkness in which a horse galloped and a gun crashed.
. . . my dead grandfather on the instant of his death" (p. 430). But
his friend Byron Bunch has realized the truth about him long before,
thinking to himself: "it's the dead folks that do him the damage. It's
the dead ones that lay quiet in one place and dont try to hold him,
that he cant escape from" (p. 65).

But Christmas has no "dead ones" to hold him, no family, no past.
The orphanage, where he was conscious that the grim old man was
watching him "all the time," and life with his foster father, the dour
Calvinist McEachern, lock him into himself. He is cut off from ties of
any sort, and he learns to suspect and resent any appeal to sentiment
or tenderness. Part of that suspicion of tenderness comes from his experiences with sex. Faulkner has most skillfully traced this development through the well-known toothpaste episode, the experience with
the Negro girl, and the affair with the prostitute-waitress Bobbie, but
he has not forced the development to extremes. Joe is not made into
an overt homosexual. But his distaste for women and his fear of them
is accounted for, and this antifeminine attitude becomes, as we shall
see, a meaningful part of the novel. It is parallel to the attitude of
Hightower, who does not understand women and comes to shrink from
them and all that they represent. Doubtless the community was
viciously wrong in accusing Hightower of homosexual practices; yet
there is a latent tendency in him just as there is in Christmas. There
is this much justice in Grimm's bitter accusation when Hightower,
attempting to give Christmas the alibi for which Bunch had pleaded,
says "He was with me the night of the murder" (p. 406).

It is Joe's latent homosexuality that involves him with Joanna Burden. When he forces himself upon her, there is "no feminine vacillation, no coyness of obvious desire. . . . It was as if he struggled physically with another man for an object of no actual value to either, and for which they struggled on principle alone" (p. 205). It is when Joanna's masculinity finally dissolves into nymphomania and that in turn gives way to feminine religiosity that Joe kills her. He cannot bear having her pray over him.

Joanna Burden is one of the most interesting of Faulkner's characters. . . . She is lonely, cut off from her kind, shunned by the community; and she has been crippled (very much as Hightower has been) by her personal inheritance. But she has courage, a quiet power of endurance, and a remarkable lack of bitterness at her plight. . . .

Joanna has been warped by the pressure of events away from the fulfillment of her nature. She has been forced to bury a part of herself; but the needs and desires are there, and when they are awakened too late for normal fulfillment in children and a home, something very terrible happens to her. Joe Christmas is perceptive enough on this point. He says to himself early in their relationship: "At least I have made a woman of her at last" (p. 207), though later, less certain of the fact, he thinks: "She's trying to be a woman and she dont know how" (p. 210). But Joe is not prepared for the torrent that is released when the "New England glacier [is] exposed suddenly to the fire of the New England biblical hell" (p. 225). Later he observes, when she sometimes stares at him "with the wild, despairing face of a stranger," that "she wants to pray, but she dont know how to do that either" (p. 228).

Faulkner is pitiless in recounting the details of Joanna's sexual discovery of herself and in indicating the man's revulsion from her—his feeling that he was "being sucked down into a bottomless morass" (p. 227). But there is never any question that Joanna is essentially the victim—of sex too long repressed, of sex driven up into the head—or of her being compelled to her actions by a self that she had scarcely known existed. To witness Joanna's one love affair is like watching a stunted autumnal plant frantically trying to bloom and seed itself before the killing frosts—"something of dying summer spurting again like a dying coal" (p. 228). Compare also: "hair just beginning to gray drawn gauntly back to a knot as savage and ugly as a wart on a diseased bough" (p. 241).

At the end, Joanna reverts to her ancestral religion—as in some sense she has known all the time that she must. "Don't make me have to pray yet," she prays. "Dear God, let me be damned a little longer, a little while" (p. 231). When she becomes once more the religious woman, the solicitous mother figure, the woman who would counsel the child and do him good, Joe finds that he has to kill her, and does —though not before Joanna has tried to kill him, for she serves a just God who will not be mocked, whose judgments are very sure, and she is ready to be that God's instrument. The last point is very important: Joanna's final gesture is not the spiteful reaction of a jilted woman. There is something almost impersonal about it. As she has told Joe when she asked him for the last time to kneel and pray with her, "It's not I who ask it" (p. 247). She is the dedicated instrument of her God, whether in saying "kneel with me" or in pulling the trigger.

Joanna Burden's frantic exploration of sex contrasts with Joe's attitude toward sex. Joe's life, as the author observes, had been, "for all its anonymous promiscuity . . . conventional enough, as a life of healthy and normal sin usually is" (p. 227). And on another level, Joanna is contrasted with Lena in her attitude toward sex, for Lena, with her uncomplicated urge to foster life, is not so much normal as an embodiment of the very norm itself.

Most of all, however, Joanna invites comparison with Hightower. Faulkner has pointed to the parallels between these two characters in a number of ways. Both are recluses. Both have been rejected by the community for good and sufficient reason. Both are dominated by the past, since the family past has impinged upon both of them in a special way. Because of all this, the incautious reader might even leap to the conclusion that it was something in the personal heritage of these two people that destroyed them, leaving them unfulfilled and incomplete. In contrast to Joe Christmas, who has no roots in anything, Joanna and Hightower may seem too deeply rooted, helplessly fettered by their personal traditions—the one of militant abolitionism, the other of the galloping Confederate cavalry leader. But neither's is a live tradition. It does not connect past with present. It is absurdly doctrinaire and abstract or absurdly romantic. That, incidentally, is how the community judges both these obsessions.

The ancestors of both Gail Hightower and Joanna Burden were able to fulfill themselves. Calvin Burden, Joanna's grandfather, was lusty, full-blooded, completely alive. He was a fire-eating abolitionist, coming home "especially on Saturday nights . . . still full of straight whiskey and the sound of his own ranting. . . . [But he] was no proselyter, [no] missionary" (p. 212). His peer is Hightower's grandfather, a "hale, bluff, rednosed man with the moustache of a brigand chief" (p. 412), triumphantly at home in his world.

Joanna's father Nathaniel, after an exciting youth spent in the Southwest, becomes an austere grizzled man who settles in Jefferson immediately after the Civil War. There his father and his son are shot down in a Reconstruction period election. But with all his justification for bitterness, and though isolated as a hated alien, he has an understanding of the values of the community. As Joanna herself reconstructs it: "We were foreigners . . . that thought differently from the people whose country we had come into without being asked or wanted. And [father] was French, half of him. Enough French to respect anybody's love for the land where he and his people were born and to understand that a man would have to act as the land where he was born had trained him to act" (p. 223).

Like Joanna's father, Hightower's father was an abolitionist, though a Southern abolitionist. But he entered the Confederate army and "took an active part in a partisan war and on the very side whose principles opposed his own" (p. 414). He taught himself surgery during the war, retained his idealism, and, as Faulkner puts it, "the other part of him, which lived in the actual world" (p. 415), was as successful as any man and more successful than most. Thus, though Joanna's and Hightower's fathers were as unlike their own fathers as they could be, they too were able to fulfill themselves. Both the grandfathers and the fathers of Joanna and Hightower were whole men, fully related to the world outside them, fully alive. The issue is not that of a Northern or Southern heritage or even that of a sensual or ascetic temperament: both traditions and both temperaments are represented in their ancestors. The real issue is whether one's relation to one's heritage permits participation in life or isolates one from life— whether it connects past with present or is simply a private obsession.

The most fascinating instance of the alienated person that occurs in the novel is that of Percy Grimm. Faulkner says: "I wrote [*Light in August*] in 1932 before I'd ever heard of Hitler's Storm Troopers," [2] and thus had described a storm trooper without knowing it. Faulkner's claim that he had described the breed without help from the newspapers is quite justified; but because of hazy and inaccurate notions of the rise of Nazism, some readers will not realize just how accurate

[2] See Frederick L. Gwynn and Joseph L. Blotner, eds., *Faulkner in the University* (Charlottesville: The University of Virginia Press, 1959), p. 41.

Faulkner's account is. In the first place, it may seem strange to them that one should regard Percy Grimm as an alienated character at all. Yet Faulkner has gone to great pains to show that Grimm is cut off from the community and is thoroughly conscious of being cut off from it. Indeed, Faulkner has been almost as careful in working up the background of Percy Grimm's spiritual starvation and alienation as he has with that of Gail Hightower.

Grimm had been born too late to take part in the First World War. Because he had missed out on being a soldier, the boy had received a kind of psychic blow. As Faulkner puts it: "The boy was suffering the terrible tragedy of having been born not alone too late but not late enough to have escaped first hand knowledge of the lost time when he should have been a man instead of a child" (p. 394). At another point, Faulkner makes the comment that Grimm had no one "to open his heart to." In short, Percy Grimm is a man who needs desperately to be felt a part of the community. He needs it so much that he attempts to seize the community values by violence. He yearns to wear a uniform marking him as the community's representative and defender. Whereas Christmas repudiates the customs and institutions of the community, Grimm insists upon seeing them in peril and demanding the right to take up arms in their defense. We shall miss the point badly if we entertain any doubts as to Percy Grimm's sincerity of motives in trying to prevent a lynching. He wants to ensure that Joe Christmas, murderer though he be, shall have a fair and proper trial.

So much for Grimm's conscious motives. What his unconscious motives are becomes plain enough when he confronts Joe Christmas at the end of the chase. Faulkner makes it clear that only in the heat of the chase does Grimm suddenly feel released, happy, fulfilled. Grimm runs "with a kind of fierce and constrained joy." Later, "above the blunt cold, rake of the automatic, his face had that serene, unearthly luminousness of angels in church windows" (p. 402). It is probably only at the very end that the dammed-up sadism is revealed even to Grimm himself, bursting forth in a full tide as he fires the shots into the overturned table and seizes the butcher knife.

A lesser artist would have made of Grimm a kind of caricature, merely brutalized and bestial. It is a mark of Faulkner's insight that even in his "Storm Trooper" he sees lurking beneath the fury and brutality the emotionally starved, lonely, terrified little boy.

In a sense we may say that Joe Christmas and Percy Grimm are closely akin—mirror images of each other in their relation to the community. This is why it makes good artistic sense that the stricken and wounded Hightower, in a final moment of truth about himself, should see the faces of Christmas and Grimm blurred together. In this vision there appear to him the faces of his wife, the townspeople, the members of his congregation, and those of Byron Bunch, Lena, and Joe Christmas. But one "face alone is not clear. It is confused more than any other, as though in the now peaceful throes of a more recent, a more inextricable, compositeness. Then he can see that it is two faces which seem to strive . . . in turn to free themselves one from the other, then fade and blend again" (p. 430). Suddenly, he realizes whose the second face is: " 'Why, it's . . .' he thinks. 'I have seen it, recently . . . Why, it's that . . . boy. . . . who fired the . . .' " (p. 431).

The theme of alienation from the community is in this novel closely connected with an emphasis on a kind of hellfire Protestantism. In much of his work Faulkner reveals himself to be a Protestant anticlerical, fascinated and also infuriated by some of the more violently repressive features of the religion that dominates his part of the country. But in *Light in August* his criticism of the harsher Protestantism is not a gratuitous gesture that disturbs the work of art: it is absorbed into the total pattern of meaning. . . .

In *Light in August* some of the characters who have become cut off from the community—and from life—become reintegrated with it, fully or partially. Such a character is Byron Bunch. He has suffered no traumatic experience in his youth; he has received no special conditioning from the past; nor has he violently rebelled or been violently rejected by the community. He is rather the methodical little "settled" man with no vices, the perpetual bachelor, who is somewhat withdrawn from the tides of life. We are told how he came to fall in love and, through this love, became involved in matters of life and death, crime and scandal. We are also told how Hightower, who had tried so desperately hard to avoid involvement ("I have brought immunity") is also drawn back into decision and responsibility. Hightower, as Bunch's confidant and in some sense his spiritual adviser, fears that Bunch is risking his "freedom," and counsels him to avoid involvement. But finally, through Bunch, he himself once more becomes involved in life and death; he delivers Lena's baby, since the doctor has not got to her in time, and he makes a desperate last-minute attempt to save Joe Christmas just before he is shot to death in the next room.

The involvement of Bunch comes through a woman, and that fact itself is significant. For the alienation of many of those separated from the community has come about through their attitudes toward

woman and sex—or at least reveals itself in those attitudes. It is so
with Christmas, with Hightower, and with Byron Bunch. One might
include Joanna Burden here, for though she is a woman, her mas-
culinization is the badge of her loneliness and the means through
which she is destroyed. Hightower makes the connection very definitely. As he passes the charred timbers of her house he says: "Poor,
barren woman. To have not lived only a week longer, until luck returned to this place. [Lena's child has just been born in a cabin on her
place.] Until luck and life returned to these barren and ruined acres"
(p. 357). Joanna's own barrenness is precisely to the point, and con-
versely Lena's fertility is connected not only literally with life but
also with luck, good fortune.

Lena, by the way, is the only one of the strangers—the outsiders
who have come into the community—who does not suffer from frustra-
tion and alienation. The others suffer from the characteristic disease
of modern life, its sick hurry and divided aims. One can recognize in
the situation of Christmas or Hightower themes characteristic of
other writers of our time such as Eliot and Joyce. To all of them one
might apply John Crowe Ransom's telling description of modern man
as a being unable "to fathom or perform his nature." Since Christmas
does not know who he is, he can express himself only in fits of compulsive violence. Gavin Stevens thinks that perhaps just before his death,
Christmas did come to know who he was, and there are rather clear
indications that Hightower fathoms his nature at the end, but this
knowledge comes very late. Lena is almost alone in not suffering from
this modern defect. She can perform her nature because she does not
need to fathom it: she *is* nature.

Lena (along with Eula of *The Hamlet*) has sometimes been called
an "earth goddess." The description does have a certain aptness when
applied to Eula, especially in some of the more rhapsodic passages of
The Hamlet. But it is a little highfalutin for Lena. It is more accurate
to say that Lena is one of Faulkner's several embodiments of the
female principle—indeed, one of the purest and least complicated of
his embodiments. Her rapport with nature is close. She is never baffled
as to what course of action to take. She is never torn by doubts and
indecisions. There is no painful introspection. This serene composure
has frequently been put down to sheer mindlessness, and Lena, to be
sure, is a very simple young woman. But Faulkner himself undoubt-
edly attributes most of Lena's quiet force to her female nature. Faulkner may indeed have had a rather romantic idea of woman. He certainly had an old-fashioned idea of her. In the Faulknerian world men

have to lose their innocence, confront the hard choice, and through a process of initiation discover reality. But women are already in possession of this knowledge, naturally and instinctively. That is why in moments of bitterness Faulkner's male characters—Mr. Compson in *The Sound and the Fury,* for example—assert that women are not innocent and have a natural affinity for evil. It would be more accurate to say that Faulkner's women lack the callow idealism of the men, have fewer illusions about human nature, and are less trammeled by legalistic distinctions and the niceties of any code.

In *Light in August,* however, the male-female contrast is stressed in a rather different way. Here, the principal male characters suffer alienation. They are separated from the community, are in rebellion against it—and against nature. But Lena moves serenely into the community and it gathers itself about her with protective gestures. Its response to her, of course, is rooted in a deep and sound instinct: Lena embodies the principle upon which any human community is founded. She is the carrier of life, and she has to be protected and nurtured if there is to be any community at all.

A basic theme in *Light in August* is man's strained attempt to hold himself up in rigid aloofness above the relaxed female world. Many of the men in the novel take up this stance, notably Hightower and Christmas. The crazed fanatic Doc Hines and the dour Presbyterian McEachern are to be numbered here too; perhaps also, though with an obvious difference, Hightower's father, Joanna Burden's father, and Joanna (as masculinized woman) herself. Byron Bunch, when we first see him, is aligned with this group. He is timid with women, and his religiousness has just a hint of the anchorite in it. Even Lucas Burch ought to be mentioned in this company—if only for comic relief (though he does have a quite literal claim to be admitted: in his own terms, he is not the marrying kind, and we last see him frantically escaping from Lena and her baby and his responsibilities to them).

Lena's function in the novel ought now to be clear. Faulkner uses her to affirm a kind of integrity and wholeness by which the alienated characters are to be judged. But Lena has more than a symbolic function. She is the means through which Byron Bunch is redeemed from his pallid half-life and brought back into the community. And she is the indirect means through which Hightower is redeemed. This coming back into the community is an essential part of their redemption. Unless the controlling purposes of the individual are related to those that other men share and in which the individual can participate, he is indeed isolated and is forced to fall back upon his personal values, with all the risk of fanaticism and distortion to which such isolation is liable.

The community is at once the field for man's action and the norm by which his action is judged and regulated. It sometimes seems that the sense of an organic community has all but disappeared from modern fiction, and the disappearance accounts for the terrifying self-consciousness and subjectivity of a great deal of modern writing. That Faulkner had some sense of an organic community still behind him was among his most important resources as a writer.

If in Faulkner's work the community can still serve as a positive norm, does that mean that in his fiction there is no room for the roles of the prophet and the saint? Can one ever find implicit approval of the individual's effort to amend or transcend the values held by the community? The answer is yes, and often. Faulkner was always fascinated by rebels and has usually accorded them a full measure of dramatic sympathy. But his fiction also reveals keen awareness of the perils risked by the individual who attempts to run counter to the community. The divergent individual may invite martyrdom; he certainly risks fanaticism and madness. In *Light in August* Faulkner's emphasis is primarily on the distortion and perversion and sterility which isolation from the community entails, though even here there is a clear recognition of a heroic element in Hightower, Joanna Burden, and Joe Christmas.

The term "redemption" may seem to claim too much for Hightower. Yet by the end of the novel he has been powerfully changed. After he has successfully delivered Lena's baby, he feels "a surge of something almost hot, almost triumphant" and thinks "I showed them! . . . Life comes to the old man yet" (p. 355). And he goes home to read not Tennyson but *Henry IV*, "food for a man" (p. 355). When he hears that Byron has left, he says to himself: "So he departed without coming to tell me goodbye" (p. 363). And then, with a conscious and purposed inversion of the usual phrase, "After all *he* has done for *me*. Fetched to me. Ay; given, restored, to me" (italics mine). Later, it is true, Hightower has to experience Christmas' attack upon him, the futile attempt to stop Grimm with a lie offered too late to save Christmas' life, and the blood-letting in his own house. But he has dared the opprobrium and told the generous lie, and in the long reverie which closes Faulkner's account of him he has admitted to himself that he "was the one who failed" (p. 426), that he was responsible for his wife's death, that he has been "a charlatan preaching worse than heresy" (p. 427), and that, bound by his romantic fixation on his grandfather's death, he has himself been neither dead nor alive. In this hour of truth he has his vision of the faces, and sees them for what they are, and he hears once again the phantom cavalry, the mystic experience with which he has sustained himself in the past, but this time he hears with a difference "the clashing sabres and the dying thunder of hooves," for he himself has finally dared something and has broken out of his self-centered dream.

Most readers have assumed that Hightower, old and exhausted, his head bandaged after Christmas' blows, dies as he hears "the dying thunder of hooves." But Faulkner, in his University of Virginia discussions, indicated that Hightower "didn't die." [3] This is obviously highly interesting; but as far as the larger scheme of the book is concerned, it hardly matters: whether Hightower died or lived on, he had broken out of the circle in which we find him at the opening of the story.

And what of Byron Bunch? Is he also "redeemed?" Can we say so in view of the curious and somewhat ambiguous ending of the novel in which Lena has not accepted marriage with Byron but, with Byron in tow, pursues her ridiculous quest for the father of her child, the unspeakable Lucas Burch? An answer to this question necessarily brings up for consideration Faulkner's attitude—not only to the characters in this episode but to all the happenings in the book. What shall we call the predominant mode? Tragic or comic or neither?

Finally and generally, I believe, the mode is that of comedy. To say so in the light of some of the terrible episodes may seem perverse. But Faulkner's comedy is frequently a makeweight to the terrible. The tender-minded reader may feel that Faulkner frequently uses a savage humor; but his is never a cynical and nihilistic humor. Its function is to maintain sanity and human perspective in a scene of brutality and horror. For example, there is the wonderful passage in which the countryman who has discovered the fire in Miss Burden's house enters and finds her body with the head almost severed, a condition which presents him with a problem in getting the dead woman downstairs. He is afraid to try to pick her up and carry her out "because her head might come clean off." But the fire forces the issue and he has to pick her up and bring her out as best he can. When he deposits the body on the ground, however, the cover in which

[3] *Ibid.*, p. 75.

he had hastily wrapped her "fell open and she was laying on her side, facing one way, and her head was turned clean around like she was looking behind her. And he said how if she could just have done that when she was alive, she might not have been doing it now" (p. 80).

This is comic and we may call it a grotesque and savage comedy, but we miss the point if we think that the countryman is being rude or cynical. It does not occur to him to leave the body in the burning house, and he has done his best under the circumstances to observe the decencies. His wry and sardonic humor is not disparaging or irreverent, though it speaks to the issue and keeps, amid the horror, a tenacious grip on common sense. Faulkner's work is full of this kind of comedy. *The Hamlet* and *As I Lay Dying* abound in it, and there is not a little of it in *Light in August*.

One can look at Faulkner's comedy in still another way. We may say that Faulkner tends to take the long view in which the human enterprise in all its basically vital manifestations is seen from far off and with great detachment. If the view is long enough and the perspective full enough, the basic attitude is almost inevitably comic. James Joyce comes to mind. His *Ulysses*, though it has much pathos and horror in it, is also finally a comic work. In *Light in August* Faulkner observes even the tragic events that involve Joanna Burden with detachment and in a full perspective. It is Lena and her instinct for nature, Lena and her rapport with the community, Lena as a link in the eternal progression from mother to daughter who provides the final norm for our judgment. In this connection Faulkner's abiding concern with man's endurance and his ability to suffer anything— compare the Nobel Prize speech—is worth remembering. Tragedy always concerns itself with the individual, his values, his tragic encounter with the reality about him, and the waste which is suffered in his defeat. Comedy involves, on the other hand, the author's basic alignment with society and with the community.

In calling *Light in August* a pastoral we have already suggested something of the comic mood. The pastoral, on the whole, aligns itself with comedy, not with tragedy. The suggestion made earlier that *Light in August* is a kind of pastoral has not been made whimsically. The last chapter of the book, with the adventures of Byron Bunch and Lena, is almost conventionally pastoral, and pastoral with an authentic comic note, for Byron is comically balked of his reward. The little man has done quite nobly. He has befriended and protected Lena, and now Lena obviously should marry him; but as the book closes, Lena is still hitchhiking across Tennessee in pursuit of Lucas Burch. Yet Byron finds it impossible to abandon her.

Our last glimpse of Lena is given through the eyes of a character whom we have not met before in the novel. Faulkner introduces him most casually. The last chapter simply opens to the statement that there lives in the eastern part of the state a furniture repairer and dealer "who recently made a trip into Tennessee to get some old pieces of furniture which he had bought by correspondence." On this trip the furniture dealer picked up the hitchhikers Lena, her baby, and her strange little bachelor companion. The oddity of the group piques his curiosity. Later he senses what is going on and the situation stirs his amusement, though it is an amusement not without insight into Lena's coquetry and not without a trace of pity for Byron's abashed devotion.

The reader may resent the casual and last-minute introduction of the new narrator and he may be disposed to dismiss this incident as simply another of Faulkner's tricky fictional devices. Yet if he has been able to see the importance of the community in this novel, he should have little difficulty in hearing and recognizing the voice of the community once more in the furniture dealer's narration. It is not important that we do not know his name or that we have not met him before or that we shall not meet him again. He can be for us the anonymous, earthy, genial, experienced, tough-minded representative of a corporate body of values, insights, and beliefs.

As such a representative, he finds Byron's plight amusing, and he obviously enjoys having so good a story to relate to his wife when he gets home. But his humor is not cruel and his insights into the relation of man and woman, the nature of chivalry, and the connection of love with honor are not untouched by a certain wisdom. In any case, we can observe that this last chapter of *Light in August,* with its comic overtones, does not really represent an abandonment of the theme that I ventured earlier to characterize in a phrase borrowed from John Crowe Ransom. For Byron Bunch too is a man unable "to fathom or perform his nature"—still unable, that is, in our last glimpse of him, to bring Lena to terms. He has acted unselfishly and gallantly, but he cannot do now what the furniture dealer knows that he ought to do: force the issue and persuade Lena to accept him as lover and husband.

On the first night they camp out together, the furniture dealer thinks that Byron has nerved himself to the act. He watches Byron quietly entering the truck where Lena is sleeping and, as he observes to his wife, "I says to myself, 'Old boy, if you'd a just done this last night, you'd a been sixty miles further south than you are now, to my knowledge" (p. 440). But Lena repels Byron's advances with the exclamation: "Why, Mr. Bunch. Aint you ashamed. You might have woke the baby, too." And the furniture dealer tells his wife: "I be dog if I dont believe she picked him up and set him back outside on the ground like she would that baby if it had been about six years old" (p. 441).

Byron had retired in confusion, but when the furniture dealer started the next day's journey with the imperturbable Lena and her child, Byron was waiting around the next curve in the road, and got back in the truck with the explanation: "I done come too far now. . . . I be dog if I'm going to quit now." Lena answers him with: "Aint nobody never said for you to quit" (p. 443).

The furniture dealer evidently has no doubt that eventually Lena will marry Byron. He says to his wife, in explaining Lena's continuation of her obviously foolish quest, "I think she was just traveling. I dont think she had any idea of finding whoever it was she was following. I dont think she had ever aimed to, only she hadn't told him [Byron] yet. . . . I reckon she knew that when she settled down this time, it would likely be for the rest of her life. That's what I think" (p. 444).

Gail Hightower, too, had earlier made the same prophecy when he imagined that Lena would continue to bear children, fulfilling her nature, but, in the future, children sired by Byron. Eventually, one supposes, Byron came to realize that Lena wanted to be possessed and mastered. For though Faulkner counsels that man should stand in awe of nature, and, loving and respecting it, should forbear to violate it, he does not expect man to stand perpetually aloof from nature, completely passive and lacking a field for action. Byron needs to learn the mean between a rape and Platonic love. But Faulkner did not choose to give us here the story of the marriage of Byron and Lena. He preferred to end his novel on the dominant theme of man's inability to fulfill himself, though the theme is treated here not tragically but with humor and amused irony—even as social comedy.

Faulkner's *Light in August*

by Michael Millgate

By comparison with *The Sound and the Fury* and *As I Lay Dying* the opening pages of *Light in August* display a much closer approximation to the techniques and progressions of "conventional" fiction. The first chapter, with its image of Lena Grove pursuing her tranquil way steadily across the face of Mississippi, immediately recalls the opening of such Hardy novels as *The Mayor of Casterbridge* or *The Return of the Native*, and even the abrupt transitions to apparently unrelated material in the second and third chapters will not disturb anyone familiar with Dickens—with, say, *Bleak House*, or *Our Mutual Friend*. Throughout *Light in August*, indeed, we are aware of an essential affinity with the major traditions of the nineteenth-century novel and especially with the work of Hardy and Dickens, and the initial impression of the relative conventionality of *Light in August* to some degree remains to the end of the book. But the demands the novel makes of its readers are by no means of a wholly conventional nature; this is especially true of the kind of moral and emotional engagement which Faulkner extorts, but it is also true of the narrative technique, which is much less straightforward than might appear at first sight.

The "time present" of the novel, as defined by the opening account of Lena's meeting with Armstid, begins on a Friday afternoon. In a sense, however, Lena's relationship with Armstid and his wife lies outside the action of the novel proper; it is a framing episode, a prelude, linked with the epilogue or coda provided in the final chapter of the book. The point at which the main action of the novel is engaged is at the very end of the first chapter, when Lena arrives on the outskirts of Jefferson and sees the smoke rising from the ruins of Miss Burden's home. This is about midday on the Saturday, and it is important to note that, for all the novel's abundance of narrative incident, many of the major events have by this time already taken place. One major event—indeed, it is one of the three crucial events in the immediate action of the novel—has taken place during the night which Lena spent at the Armstids': this is the death of Joanna Burden. The two other crucial events both take place on the ninth day following Lena's arrival in Jefferson; that Monday morning Lena gives birth to her child, and that afternoon Percy Grimm hunts down Joe Christmas and kills him. A very considerable proportion of the novel is taken up with extended "flashbacks" which recount the history of various characters up to the point at which they become involved in the present action. . . .

. . . We first see Christmas, for example, as he appears to Mooney, the foreman at the planing mill, to Byron Bunch, and to the people of Jefferson generally: only later are we given those details of Christmas's birth and upbringing which force us radically to amend our judgment of a man whom we, like the people of Jefferson, have already condemned on sight as inherently vicious and worthless. . . . If, on the other hand, we are given Lena Grove's history the moment she appears, that is primarily because she and her background are so simple and so easily explained, and because she seems not so much a character in the book, with possibilities of development and unanticipated variety, as a kind of impersonalised catalytic force, effecting change but itself unchanging. She provides a steady, imperturbable groundnote, an onward linear progression that offers a constant contrast to the desperate contortions—moral, emotional, and physical—of the other characters.

It seems possible to speak almost in diagrammatic terms of this novel, rich as it is in symbolic potentialities, disposed in large and readily distinguishable blocks of material, and with whole scenes presented almost in the form of tableaux, as formalised, even frozen, action:[1] Lena traversing the face of Mississippi "like something moving forever and without progress across an urn" (p. 5); Christmas and McEachern waiting in rigid immobility during the intervals of their

---

[1] See Darrel Abel, "Frozen Movement in *Light in August*," *Boston University Studies in English*, III (Spring 1957), 32–44 [this volume, pp. 42–54]; Norman Holmes Pearson, "Lena Grove," *Shenandoah*, III (Spring 1952), 3–7.

hourly ritual of command, refusal, and punishment; Percy Grimm pursuing Christmas "with that lean, swift, blind obedience to whatever Player moved him on the Board" (p. 437). It is remarkable that a great deal even of the present action of the novel is not directly recounted but reflected in the minds and memories of witnesses who were not themselves involved in the action: Gavin Stevens giving his interpretation of the events leading to Christmas's death; the furniture dealer telling his wife of his encounter with Lena and Byron Bunch; the impersonal "they" of the latter part of Chapter 15, recounting "about supper tables in electrically lighted rooms and in remote hill cabins with kerosene lamps" (p. 330) the story of Christmas's arrest in Mottstown and the curious behaviour of Doc Hines and his wife. It is almost as though Faulkner were seeking to "domesticate," to incorporate within the structure of a conventional novel, the technique of multiple reflection which he had earlier employed in *As I Lay Dying,* and it is certainly clear that in *Light in August* he is concerned not merely to tell the stories of Joe Christmas, Lena Grove and Gail Hightower but also, and perhaps primarily, to show the impact of these stories upon the people of Jefferson.

One cannot avoid speaking in the plural of the stories of Christmas, Lena and Hightower, for there are quite unmistakably three distinct strands in the novel. They are not, however, entirely separable strands, and critics have become steadily more aware of the essential unity of the novel, a unity secured through various forms of thematic interrelation and ironic reflection rather than through the more familiar kinds of narrative link—though even these links are stronger and more numerous than has often been allowed, as Malcolm Cowley discovered when he attempted to separate one of the strands for inclusion in *The Portable Faulkner.*[2] Joanna Burden, in the corruption of a sensuality discovered too late and pursued too far, offers an obvious contrast to the healthy animality of Lena Grove; Lena herself, travelling down her "peaceful corridor paved with unflagging and tranquil faith and peopled with kind and nameless faces and voices," (p. 4) is at the opposite pole from Joe Christmas, who for fifteen years has travelled down a street which "ran on in its moods and phases, always empty: he might have seen himself as in numberless avatars, in silence, doomed

---

[2] Malcolm Cowley to William Faulkner, September 17, 1945. The Faulkner-Cowley correspondence is deposited in the Yale University Library. Faulkner's letters are, with one exception, undated but have been numbered and catalogued in the sequence in which Malcolm Cowley placed them. Future references will give simply this number.

with motion, driven by the courage of flagged and spurred despair."
(p. 213) Faulkner himself spoke of Hightower as the antithesis of
Christmas, in that he "escaped into his past," [3] presumably an allusion
to the way in which Christmas, bereft of all certainty about his past,
cannot rest from his passionate engagement with the present. On a
more comic level, there is the utter dichotomy between the conscien-
tious Byron Bunch and his shiftless "rival" and near-namesake, Lucas
Burch. . . .

Running throughout the book is that fundamental irony which
Faulkner explores to a greater or lesser degree in almost all of his
novels: the gulf between appearance and actuality, the contrast between the public and the private self. We have already noted the contrast between the outward face of Joe Christmas and the inner reality
with which the reader becomes increasingly familiar as the book pro-
gresses. Another character whom we apprehend on two levels in this
way is Joanna Burden, inwardly a chaos of sensuality, outwardly a
woman of mature wisdom, dispensing "advice, business, financial and
religious, to the presidents and faculties and trustees, and advice personal and practical to young girl students and even alumnae, of a
dozen negro schools and colleges through the south." (p. 20) Hightower and Byron Bunch are other characters in whom we become aware
of such a duality, while again and again we realise that the characters
themselves are seeing their fellow men and women not as they actually
are but as they wish them to be: so Miss Burden sees Christmas as
"negro"; so Hightower discerns in his wife, as Joe Christmas discerns
in Bobbie Allen, a non-existent quality of love.

These ironic patterns are clearly related to that theme in the novel
which critics have often, and rightly, identified as being of major significance: the demand of organised society and organised religion that
the human individual act in strict accordance with prescribed abstract
patterns. At the hands of religious authoritarians such as Hines and
McEachern, Christmas has suffered all his life from this demand, and it
is in response to the same rigid requirement that he is finally hunted
down according to the rules prescribed in Jefferson for the treatment of
"nigger murderers." There are, too, several passages in the novel which
seem to imply a general social denunciation. After the death of Miss
Burden, for instance, the people of Jefferson refused to let her body
lie in peace but preferred to believe that it "cried out for vengeance"
(p. 273) . . . It is interesting, however, that Faulkner's criticism of

---

[3] Frederick L. Gwynn and Joseph L. Blotner, eds., *Faulkner in the University*
(Charlottesville: The University of Virginia Press, 1959), p. 45.

Jefferson is relatively mild. After the arrest of Christmas it is the peace and quiet of the town which is insisted upon: Percy Grimm walks across "the quiet square empty of people peacefully at suppertables about that peaceful town and that peaceful country," (p. 430) and Faulkner makes it entirely clear in this deeply imagined and superbly evoked episode that it is Percy Grimm alone who provokes the town to that course of ritual action of which he himself inevitably becomes the final instrument. The men who share Grimm's pursuit of Christmas do not necessarily share his savagery, for one of them vomits at the sight of the castration, and it is clear that, in his presentation of Grimm, Faulkner was not especially concerned to portray a specifically Southern type of violence: years later he wrote to Malcolm Cowley of having created a Nazi before Hitler did.[4] Although it would be an exaggeration to say that in its conduct towards Christmas the society of Jefferson appears at its collective worst, it might at least be said that the occasion permitted the worst elements in Jefferson to emerge and take command. But in any case a counterbalance is supplied by Lena Grove: she brings out—not always readily, but eventually—the best in Jefferson, and it is with Lena, in her familiar role as the calm recipient of kindness, that the book begins and ends.

There is, however, little qualification or amelioration of the book's rejection of organised religion and religious fanaticism. The bigotry of several characters, in the past as well as the present, is closely examined and shown to be self-condemned by its own rigidity and inhumanity, and it is a final astringent touch in Faulkner's treatment of this theme that as Percy Grimm hunts down Joe Christmas his face displays "that serene, unearthly luminousness of angels in church windows," (p. 437) and his voice sounds "clear and outraged like that of a young priest." (p. 439) All these characters, so assured in their narrow faith, are in contrast to Joe Christmas himself, a man engaged in unceasing introspection, a persistent and desperate search for personal identity and for a meaning in life.[5] He is several times likened to a monk, and Faulkner, answering a question put to him at the University of Virginia, spoke revealingly of Christmas's self-isolation from the world . . .[6] For all his confusion, however, it is Christmas who discovers one of the two

[4] Malcolm Cowley, Editor's Note, *The Portable Faulkner* (New York: The Viking Press, 1946), p. 652. Compare Faulkner to Cowley, 9.

[5] See Alfred Kazin, "The Stillness of *Light in August*," in Frederick J. Hoffman and Olga W. Vickery, eds., *William Faulkner: Three Decades of Criticism* (New York and Burlingame: Harcourt, Brace and World, Inc., 1963), pp. 252–53.

[6] Gwynn and Blotner, eds., *Faulkner in the University*, p. 72. [See Faulkner's own discussion of Joe Christmas on pp. 93–94, 95 of this volume.]

forms of religious and moral experience which Faulkner appears to offer as valid. Christmas, who becomes godlike in his last agony, discovers the way of suffering, of passive acceptance, the path of crucifixion. The opposite but complementary figure in the novel is Lena Grove, who, in her simple and unquestioning acceptance of a kind of natural religion, seems to embody those simple and permanent values which Faulkner so frequently and so powerfully affirmed, the values of endurance, patience, fecundity, and simple faith. *"That will be her life, her destiny,"* Hightower recognises: *"The good stock peopling in tranquil obedience to it the good earth; from these hearty loins without hurry or haste descending mother and daughter."* (p. 384)

The opposition, and indeed counterpoint, of Lena Grove and Joe Christmas is clear and apparent throughout the novel, and its validity is readily acceptable. The disturbing figure, morally and structurally, is that of Hightower. He has seemed to many critics a shadowy and indeterminate figure, lacking a sufficiently substantial stake in the plot or an adequately defined role in the moral or symbolic patterns of the book as a whole. But such a judgment may result from a failure to distinguish Hightower's functions from Faulkner's deliberate characterisation of him as a non-participator, a man withdrawn from life and its sufferings. . . .

*   *   *

. . . The "idea" in forming Faulkner's presentation of Hightower is clear; it is, indeed, sufficiently implied in the obvious symbolism of his name.[7] But Hightower . . . has . . . more than a merely narrative connection with the Byron Bunch-Lena Grove relationship. He is more than once described as an eastern idol, and for Byron Bunch he is initially a repository of wisdom; it is Byron who interprets the stale smell of Hightower's house as the odour of goodness. Byron at the opening of the book is Hightower's disciple, his imitator in silence, withdrawal, isolation from life; but Byron is converted by his love for Lena to a new concern for humanity which soon extends beyond his relationship with Lena herself and overflows into a compassionate if hopeless attempt to aid Joe Christmas. What vitiates so many of the relationships in the novel—between Joanna Burden and Joe Christmas, for example, between Christmas and his various women, between Hightower and his wife—is their selfishness and lack of generosity: the

---

[7] Mr. Albert Erskine has pointed out to me, however, that the name is not uncommon in Mississippi.

partners use those whom they claim to love primarily as a means of attacking some personal problem. As Hightower comes eventually to realise of his own married life, such relationships remain on an abstract level rather than a human one, and they are effectively criticised in terms of the warm, humane, and outward-going quality of Byron's love for Lena. Byron not only breaks with his earlier discipleship but actually becomes his master's teacher, showing him the way to that recognition of value in life, in human involvement, which Hightower finally achieves. It is, however, too late for Hightower to be effectively reborn. Lena does not name her baby after him, and his mind cannot rest in the vision of human solidarity and interdependence which he has with such agony achieved but returns ineluctably to that obsessive image of his grandfather which has haunted him throughout his life— though Faulkner himself reminded us that this image was not in itself an ignoble one: "[Hightower] had to endure, to live, but that was one thing that was pure and fine that he had—was the memory of his grandfather, who had been brave." [8]

Faulkner said more than once that he began *Light in August* with nothing clearly in mind save the image of Lena Grove—"knowing no more about it than a young woman, pregnant, walking along a strange country road." [9] . . . The suggestion that "Light in August" is a countryman's expression used of a cow or mare due to drop her calf or foal in that month might tend to confirm the primacy of the Lena Grove element, but it seems unlikely that in choosing a title for so various a novel Faulkner would have such a narrow range of relevance in mind.[10] In any case, discussion of this point has to some extent diverted attention from other substantial justifications for the title which appear within the book itself. Many critics have noticed the frequency in the novel of images of light and dark, for example, and Faulkner spoke very interestingly of a special quality of light which he had in mind:

> [I]n August in Mississippi there's a few days somewhere about the middle of the month when suddenly there's a foretaste of fall, it's cool, there's a lambence, a luminous quality to the light, as though it came not from just today but from back in the old classic times. It might have fauns and satyrs and the gods and—from Greece, from Olympus in it some-

[8] Gwynn and Blotner, eds., *Faulkner in the University,* p. 75; see also p. 45.

[9] Typescript of an unpublished autobiographical piece in the Alderman Library, pp. 2–3.

[10] The manuscript in the Alderman Library seems originally to have been entitled "Dark House" . . . possibly an allusion to section VII of Tennyson's *In Memoriam.*

where. It lasts just for a day or two, then it's gone, but every year in
August that occurs in my country, and that's all that title meant, it was
just to me a pleasant evocative title because it reminded me of that time,
of a luminosity older than our Christian civilization.[11]

It is this light which shines on the day of Christmas's death and at the
moment when Hightower finally recognises the truth about himself and
the extent of his responsibility both for his own suffering and for that
of his dead wife: "In the lambent suspension of August into which
night is about to fully come, it [the wheel of his thinking] seems to engender and surround itself with a faint glow like a halo." (p. 465) But
Faulkner seems to hint at some wider meaning in his references to "the
old classic times . . . fauns and satyrs and the gods" and the "pagan
quality" of Lena Grove. The "earth-mother" qualities in Lena Grove
are clearly hinted at in her name, and have long been recognised. But
given Faulkner's undoubted familiarity with these stories of classical
mythology and with the works of Joyce and Eliot, and his probable
acquaintance with Frazer's *The Golden Bough,* it would not be sur-
prising if he had further analogies in mind: not necessarily a complex
and carefully articulated pattern of analogy such as Joyce evolved in
Ulysses, but perhaps some slightly opportunistic exploitation of an
available source such as he had shown in his allocation of three sections
of *The Sound and the Fury* to the dates of Easter 1929 or in the various
hinted analogies in *Light in August* itself between Joe Christmas and
Jesus Christ, between Lena Grove and the Virgin Mary, and between
Byron Bunch and Mary's husband, Joseph.[12]

Any search for underlying patterns in *Light in August* might well
begin with a consideration of the extensive series of parallels and sub-
stitutions which appear in the course of the novel and which again
and again establish thematic and even narrative links between its different strands. An obvious example is Mrs. Hines's confused identification of Lena's baby with Joe Christmas when he was a child, and her
further reference to the baby as being actually Christmas's son.[13] One
thinks also of the similarities between the apparently opposed back-
grounds of Hightower and Miss Burden, fanatics of the South and of

[11] Gwynn and Blotner, eds., *Faulkner in the University,* p. 199.

[12] See Robert M. Slabey, "Myth and Ritual in *Light in August,*" *Texas Studies in
Literature and Language,* II (Autumn 1960), 328–49 [this volume, pp. 91–92], for
an extremely interesting discussion of mythic elements in the novel.

[13] Kazin, "The Stillness of *Light in August,*" p. 249, speaks of this incident as
"virtually an annunciation."

the North; of the parallelism between the tragic encounter of Joe Christmas with Percy Grimm and the primarily comic encounter of Byron Bunch with Lucas Burch, which takes place at the same moment in time; of the reverberations set up in the reader's mind by the incident of Christmas breaking into a Negro church like an impersonation of the devil, recalling as it does both the mad forays into Negro churches made by his grandfather, Doc Hines, and the moment of Satanic glee caught by the camera as Hightower leaves his empty church.

Most important of all, however, is the relationship between Miss Burden and Lena Grove and Lena's replacement of Miss Burden at the plantation after the latter's death, and there are reasons for thinking that Faulkner may have intended a series of allusions to the goddess Diana and to the sacred groves where she was worshipped. Lena Grove's name is an obvious hint leading in this direction, and the Burden house itself is several times described as standing almost hidden among a grove of trees, a grove which still stands even when the house itself has gone; the place, too, is one to which Negro women have come for many years as to a shrine or to a "wise woman"—"approaching the house in a manner not exactly secret, yet purposeful, . . . emerging again and returning down the radiating paths not fast and yet not loitering." (p. 243) Miss Burden, the original mistress of the grove, is not on the face of it an especially Diana-like character, but she has certain characteristics in common with the Roman Diana— notably her masculinity, her reputation for virginity, and her moon-like ebb and flow of passion as she and Christmas pass through all the different phases of their relationship—and it is she whom the Negro women have consulted in their troubles, especially, it appears (p. 251), in those troubles of pregnancy and childbirth which were Diana's special province. Lena Grove, on the other hand, with her name, her air of timeless permanence, and her fecundity, has much in common with that Ephesian Diana who was specifically an earth-mother, fertility figure.

Is there, perhaps, some sense in which Faulkner intended the ritualistic murder of Joanna Burden, carried out as Lena Grove pauses overnight on the outskirts of the town, to be an act preparatory to the replacement of Miss Burden's alien, outmoded, and sterile influence by the natural vitality and fecundity embodied in Lena? Certainly something more than the mere establishment of a weak narrative link seems to be involved in Lena's occupation of the cabin on the Burden estate and the birth there of her child. Hightower, in particular, makes it clear that new life has come to the run-down plantation, the "ruined garden," (p. 264) that some kind of symbolic rebirth has been enacted:

> He emerges from the woods at the far side of the pasture behind the cabin. Beyond the cabin he can see the clump of trees in which the house had stood and burned, though from here he cannot see the charred and mute embers of what were once planks and beams. "Poor woman," he thinks. "Poor, barren woman. To have not lived only a week longer, until luck returned to this place. Until luck and life returned to these barren and ruined acres." It seems to him that he can see, feel, about him the ghosts of rich fields, and of the rich fecund black life of the quarters, the mellow shouts, the presence of fecund women, the prolific naked children in the dust before the doors; and the big house again, noisy, loud with the treble shouts of the generations. (p. 385)

Hightower sees the pathos of Miss Burden's passing, but the reader may sense that her death has in some way been a precondition of the rebirth which is here so eloquently evoked. The death seems fated, like so much else in the novel, and, like the death of Joe Christmas nine days later, it is certainly executed in ritualistic fashion: Miss Burden herself prepares for it in prayer and Christmas prepares for it by performing what can perhaps be best described as the quasi-rituals of stripping himself of the last woman-sewn button and showing himself naked in the lights of a passing car, by shaving at the spring, and by temporarily immersing himself in the "thick black pit" (p. 107) of the Negro district.

Immediately before Christmas goes in to kill Miss Burden, at midnight on the Friday, we are given this insight into his thoughts:

> Now it was still, quiet, the fecund earth now coolly suspirant. The dark was filled with the voices, myriad, out of all time that he had known, as though all the past was a flat pattern. And going on: tomorrow night, all the tomorrows, to be a part of the flat pattern, going on. He thought of that with quiet astonishment: going on, myriad, familiar, since all that had ever been was the same as all that was to be, since tomorrow to-be and had-been would be the same. Then it was time. (p. 266)

This is as precise a verbal definition as can be found in the novel of the kind of representative significance embodied by Lena Grove: Christmas here realises, in a flash of insight, the fundamental permanence of the earth and of human experience which lies beneath and beyond the immediate present of agonised searching and violent experience in which he is himself so inextricably engaged. Also significant, however, is the final statement: "Then it was time." This is the moment on which, in a very real sense, the whole novel turns, the moment of midnight on the Friday night which Lena spends at the Armstids'. It is on this point of time that the entire long flashback recounting Christmas's previous experiences is poised, and since the flashback begins on page 111 and occupies only a few pages short of a third of the novel, it must be considered one of Faulkner's most extended experiments in suspended time.

The statement, "Then it was time," may thus be in the nature of an announcement that the moment has been released from its suspension, that the action is henceforward immersed once more in the flow of time. This is, however, a novel in which the course of present events is very carefully charted and in which many of the characters display an extraordinary awareness of time: Byron meticulously keeps his own time when working alone; Hightower always knows the time although he has no clock; while Christmas is being pursued he is driven to speak to people not by any need for food but by his need to know what day it is. It seems probable that Faulkner had some kind of deliberate time scheme in mind as he wrote the book, and since the ancient festival of Diana used to be celebrated in August it is conceivable that he intended some allusion to it.[14] The fact that fire was especially important in the celebration of the festival would then give additional significance to the fire at the Burden house and to the title of the novel itself. There are several more hints of this kind, and there are even a number of features in the account of Christmas's pursuit and murder by Percy Grimm—most notably, the comparison of Grimm to a young priest—which tempt one to wonder whether Faulkner's imagination may not initially have been seized by Frazer's description in the opening pages of *The Golden Bough* of the "barbarous custom" followed in Roman times to decide the succession to the priesthood of Diana's sacred grove and sanctuary at Nemi.[15]

These suggested correspondences between *Light in August* and the mythology and anthropology surrounding the figure of Diana may be entirely accidental. Alternatively, such correspondences, like those

[14] J. G. Frazer, *The Golden Bough: A Study in Magic and Religion* (London, 1911), Part I, Vol. 1, pp. 12–14. The present action of *Light in August* apparently takes place in 1932 (see William H. F. Lamont, "The Chronology of *Light in August*," *Modern Fiction Studies*, III [Winter 1957–1958], 360–361), and it is perhaps worth noting that in that year August 13, the date of Diana's festival, fell on a Saturday: Joe Christmas waits for midnight on the Friday night before going into the house to kill Miss Burden in the early moments of the Saturday.

[15] Frazer, *The Golden Bough*, Part I, Vol. 1, pp. 8–11.

linking characters in the book with the members of the Holy Family, may represent only one among several patterns of analogy which Faulkner pursued in the course of the novel, and it is possible that he intended a symbolic substitution of Lena as a Holy Mother figure (an aspect in her presentation which is particularly stressed in the final chapter) for the barren Diana figure of Miss Burden.[16] But one thing is clear: the structure of *Light in August* cannot be adequately defined as a loose combination and conflation of three separate stories. As other critics have argued, there are in effect three quite distinct conclusions to the novel, each containing a bare minimum of references to the other two, and it would have been extremely simple for Faulkner, had he so wished, to establish a much closer texture of purely narrative links between the three strands. He did not so choose, however, and the structure of *Light in August* which we have already remarked as harking back in certain important respects to *As I Lay Dying* may also be said to look forward to the divided "double-novel" structure of *The Wild Palms*. But in reading *Light in August* we are not especially aware of the discreteness of the different narrative strands. Much of the novel's cohesion derives from its interconnecting patterns of reflection, repetition, substitution, and contrast. Something is also gained by Faulkner's use of recurrent images, such as that of the circle, and of analogical patterns. But the great and unifying strength of the book remains its most obvious one: the sheer force and passion of its presentation of Joe Christmas, the quintessential victim, and the way in which we, like all the characters in the book, are irresistibly swept into the vortex of Christmas's restless life and agonising death.

[16] Compare *ibid.*, p. 14: "The Christian Church appears to have sanctified this great festival of the Assumption of the Blessed Virgin on the fifteenth of August." This first chapter of *The Golden Bough* offers many extremely suggestive points of comparison with *Light in August*.

PART TWO

View Points

THE BROADER DESIGN
OF FAULKNER'S FICTION

William Faulkner

As regards any specific book, I'm trying primarily to tell a story, in the most effective way I can think of, the most moving, the most exhaustive. But I think even that is incidental to what I am trying to do, taking my output (the course of it) as a whole. . . .

Malcolm Cowley

Faulkner's mythical kingdom is a county in northern Mississippi, on the border between the sand hills covered with scrubby pine and the black earth of the river bottoms. Except for the storekeepers, mechanics, and professional men who live in Jefferson, the county seat, all the inhabitants are farmers or woodsmen. Except for a little lumber, their only product is baled cotton for the Memphis market. A few of them live in big plantation houses, the relics of another age, and more of them in substantial wooden farmhouses; but most of them are tenants, no better housed than slaves on good plantations before the Civil War. Yoknapatawpha County—"William Faulkner, sole owner and proprietor," as he inscribed on one of the maps he drew—has a population of 15,611 persons scattered over 2,400 square miles. It sometimes seems to me that . . . all the people of the imaginary county, black and white, townsmen, farmers, and housewives, have played their parts in one connected story. . . .

All his books in the Yoknapatawpha saga are part of the same living pattern. It is this pattern, and not the printed volumes in which part of it is recorded, that is Faulkner's real achievement. Its existence helps to explain one feature of his work: that each novel, each long or short story, seems to reveal more than it states explicitly and to have a subject bigger than itself.

THE UNITY OF *Light in August*

Malcolm Cowley

"Light in August" I now feel is the best of your novels. . . . I thought when I first read it that it dissolved too much into the three separate stories of Lena Grove (wonderful), Hightower and Joe Christmas—but I read it [again] with the idea that Lena or Joe might be picked out of the text and found that they were too closely interwoven with the others. It would be easy for you to *write* Joe Christmas into a separate novel, but the anthologist can't pick him out without leaving bits of his flesh hanging to Hightower and Lena.

From Malcolm Cowley, Letter to William Faulkner [September 17, 1945], in Malcolm Cowley, The Faulkner-Cowley File: Letters and Memories *(New York: The Viking Press, Inc., 1966), pp. 28–29. Copyright © 1966 by Malcolm Cowley. Excerpted and reprinted with the permission of The Viking Press, Inc., and Chatto & Windus Ltd.*

Lawrance Thompson

One element of form has been saved for a final consideration. It is the structural antithesis of counterpoint established between the story of what happened to Joe Christmas and the story of what happened to

---

From William Faulkner: An Introduction and Interpretation, *by Lawrance Thompson, Second Edition. Copyright © 1963, 1967 by Holt, Rinehart and Winston, Inc. Excerpted and reprinted by permission of Holt, Rinehart and Winston, Inc.*

Lena Grove. One aspect of theme acquires implicit illumination from Faulkner's arrangement of those two narratives in such a way that the action starts and ends with Lena Grove. Here, as in *The Sound and the Fury*, the structural arrangement lets the positives bracket and contain the negatives. Lena Grove is another of Faulkner's primitive and pagan characters; a social outcast who has made herself vulnerable to social criticism because she has violated certain moral conventions. At first glance, her innocent attitudes toward love and hate appear to be merely naïve. Yet from the start Lena Grove is represented as having a peculiar power to evoke from others various reflections of her own gentleness, kindliness, and compassion. Implicitly, Faulkner establishes an important counterpoint between Lena Grove's capacity for placing herself in accord with "the old earth of and with and by which she lives," and Joe Christmas' placing himself at odds with "the very immutable laws which earth must obey." If interpreted within the framework of Faulkner's moral vision, those "laws" have to do with the "verities of the heart." They include an awareness of the practical necessity implicit in positive expressions of courage, endurance, compassion, aspiration, sacrifice, pride, and love. Faulkner begins by establishing her pagan kinship with Mother Earth and with the fruitful light of August: "swollen, slow, deliberate, unhurried and tireless as augmenting afternoon itself . . . with that providential caution of the old earth of and with and by which she lives." The analogies implied between her inner light and the outer light of August becomes reinforced when Hightower says of her, after her child has been born on the morning of the day Joe Christmas is to die, "That will be her life, her destiny. The good stock peopl[ing], in tranquil obedience to it, the good earth; from these hearty loins without hurry or haste descending mother and daughter." Those passages suggest why Faulkner chose to bracket, structurally, the negations and hatreds of the Joe Christmas story within the affirmations of the Lena Grove story.

PROTESTANTISM AS ANTAGONIST IN
Light in August

William Van O'Connor

[William Faulkner saw the] Protestant or puritan spirit as . . . one of the most significant factors, even the key factor, in the tragedy of

Negro and white relationships. This theme [is] . . . explicitly worked out and elaborated in . . . *Light in August*. If one does not perceive that the Calvinist spirit is the central issue of *Light in August*, the novel of necessity will seem confused in theme. It is episodic in structure, but the meaning is clear. The Civil War and the black shadow of slavery do, as some critics insist, suffuse the book. It is proper enough to observe the position of Hightower in the story, to relive with him the imagined scenes of galloping horses, burning buildings, the wounded and dead of the Civil War—these do live on into the 1920's, even in the minds of those less crippled by such memories than the defrocked old minister. But the greater force, in which the War and the black shadow are caught up, is Calvinism, and, larger than it, rigidity of principle and harshness of spirit; and it is this force that menaces Joe Christmas, the putative Negro, and that persecutes Hightower. Byron Bunch and Lena Grove are more than comic relief; they are proof that one need not succumb to such a force.

From *"Protestantism in Yoknapatawpha County"* by *William Van O'Connor,* The Hopkins Review, *V* (*Spring, 1952*), *31. Excerpted and reprinted with the permission of the publisher.*

Hyatt H. Waggoner

In one of Gail Hightower's final meditations he pronounces an often quoted judgment on Southern Protestant Christianity. The music he hears coming from the church seems to him to have "a quality stern and implacable, deliberate and without passion so much as immolation, pleading, asking, for not love, not life, forbidding it to others, demanding in sonorous tones death, as though death were the boon, like all Protestant music." "Puritanism," or punitive religious moralism, is perhaps the chief intended antagonist in *Light in August,* as it is the immediate antagonist in *Sanctuary.*

"Pleasure, ecstasy," Hightower thinks, "they cannot seem to bear." Hines and McEachern could be his illustrations, the two most obviously pious people in the story and the two most responsible for the fate of Joe Christmas. He does not think of them because he does not know what we know about Christmas's past, but we, reading, supply

From William Faulkner: From Jefferson to the World *by Hyatt H. Waggoner* (*Lexington: University of Kentucky Press, 1959*), *pp. 100–101. Excerpted and reprinted with the permission of the publisher.*

them for him. And when we have finished the novel we feel that events have proved Hightower right when he pictures a crucifixion inflicted not despite but because of the religion of his fellow townsmen:

> *And so why should not their religion drive them to crucifixion of themselves and one another?* . . . It seems to him that the past week has rushed like a torrent and that the week to come, which will begin tomorrow, is the abyss, and that now on the brink of the cataract the stream has raised a single blended and sonorous and austere cry, not for justification but as a dying salute before its own plunge, and not to any god but to the doomed man in the barred cell within hearing of them and of the two other churches, and in whose crucifixion they too will raise a cross. "And they will do it gladly," he says, in the dark window.

Hightower's thoughts constitute a terrible indictment of Southern Christianity, charging that it has become so distorted that it leads men toward hatred and destruction and death, crucifying Christ all over again, and "gladly." A great deal of the substance of the book has the effect of leading us to accept this judgment, and *Light in August* is Faulkner's most fully documented statement on what he sees as the religious errors and the racist guilt of his region. The grim fanatical fundamentalism of McEachern and the mad fundamentalist racism of Hines are judged in negative terms and without any shadow of qualification.

Lawrance Thompson

[A]ny statement of Faulkner's major thematic concerns in *Light in August* should point out that in none of his other novels does Faulkner unburden himself quite so furiously as to what he believes to be certain aberrations in Christian practice. He might even be giving conscious support to Nietzsche's claim that Christianity has found ways for poisoning human strength and dignity through preaching excessive self-contempt and self-immolation. A careful reading of *Light in August* should clarify the fact that the basic antithesis or counterpoint or polarity, here, is derived from Faulkner's rebellious insistence on contrasting certain pagan attitudes with certain Christian attitudes for

From William Faulkner: An Introduction and Interpretation, *by Lawrance Thompson, Second Edition. Copyright © 1963, 1967 by Holt, Rinehart and Winston, Inc. Excerpted and reprinted by permission of Holt, Rinehart and Winston, Inc.*

purposes of honoring the pagan. Whatever concepts Faulkner here salvages from his own Christian heritage he reinterprets, as a means of separating them from those meanings in Christian dogma. If he chose largely to define the positive elements of his themes in terms of negatives, he may have done so because once again he wanted to shock, hurt, and upset Christian complacencies.

Sex and Women in *Light in August*

Maxwell Geismar

. . . Faulkner's eroticism is in the end hardly erotic. The underlying view is not sexual, but a distaste for sex. It retards rather than arouses the sensual impulses, throws its blight, in fact, over all the natural passions . . . [with its] emphasis on necrophilia and cannibalism, on misogynists and miscegenation, . . . [on] murderers and their dangling corpses, . . . "Light in August" appears to synthesize all the strains of Faulkner's discontent.

In its scope "Light in August" is certainly one of Faulkner's big novels. Here he has again penetrated more deeply into his people and created a more complex scene than that of "As I Lay Dying." Here too, in a curious way, Faulkner is closer to the central figures of his novel, though it is not easy at first for us to recognize just who the central figures of the novel are. Written as objective narrative rather than interior monologue, "Light in August" is still not without complexity in its exposition. Through the story of Lena, another poor-white mountain girl, again pregnant, again wandering, again seeking the father of her child, and again, we are inclined to believe, mentally deficient, we come to Byron Bunch who falls in love with her. Through Byron's story, we come to Hightower, the minister, betrayed by his wife, driven out of his parish by his congregation, living in disgrace with the town and among his memories of the Civil War. Caught by the dead who had conceived him, the son "who grew to manhood among phantoms" dies among them—

From "William Faulkner: The Negro and the Female," Writers in Crisis: The American Novel, 1925–1940 *by Maxwell Geismar (Boston: Houghton Mifflin Company, 1942), pp. 162–64. Excerpted and reprinted with the permission of the publisher.*

He hears above his heart the thunder increase, myriad and drumming. Like a long sighing of wind in trees it begins, they sweep into sight, borne now upon a cloud of phantom dust. They rush past, forwardleaning in the saddles, with brandished arms, beneath whipping ribbons from slanted and eager lances; with tumult and soundless yelling they sweep past . . . are gone; the dust swirls skyward sucking, fades away into the night which has fully come. Yet . . . it seems to him that he still hears them: the wild bugles and the clashing sabres and the dying thunder of hooves.

From the story of Hightower, held by that moment of thundering hooves and wild bugles in which his life, Faulkner tells us, had begun and ended, we come at last (I am simplifying the exposition, since these narratives within narratives are also broken in time and place) to the murder in Jefferson. Working backward in time from that, we reach the relationship of Joe Christmas and the Miss Burden of "Light in August." And what a romance this is, the central love affair of Faulkner's maturity—this colored Romeo and abolitionist Juliet of Jefferson, Mississippi; the amoral mulatto and the starved spinster; the brutal criminal and the aging nymphomaniac. We come at last to the vicious conjunction in Faulkner's work of the Negro and the Female, the twin furies of Faulkner's deep southern Waste Land; but a waste land, quite unlike Eliot's, of demons and incubae rather than pallid clerks, one which is built on diseased fury and ends, indeed, not with a whimper but a bang.

Which of these entwined partners of evil seems to earn more of Faulkner's opprobrium? It is the woman, Faulkner implies, who has been responsible for the fate of Joe Christmas, the new Faulknerian hero, orphan and outcast, hunted by the world and venting his own hatred on it, semblance of a white man who carried the taint of his own knowledge that he is negro. It is worth while noticing the sequence of female actions which have conditioned the history of Christmas.

Leslie A. Fiedler

In the work of William Faulkner, the fear of the castrating woman and the dis-ease with sexuality present in the novels of his contem-

From Love and Death in the American Novel *by Leslie A. Fiedler (New York: Stein & Day Publishers, 1966), pp. 320–22. Copyright © 1966, 1960 by Leslie A. Fiedler. Excerpted and reprinted with the permission of Stein & Day Publishers, and Jonathan Cape Ltd.*

poraries, Fitzgerald and Hemingway, attain their fullest and shrillest
expression. Not content with merely projecting images of the anti-
virgin, he insists upon editorializing against the woman he travesties
in character and situation. No Jiggs and Maggie cliché of popular
anti-feminism is too banal for him to use; he reminds us (again and
again!) that men are helpless in the hands of their mothers, wives,
and sisters; that females do not think but proceed from evidence to
conclusions by paths too devious for males to follow; that they possess
neither morality nor honor; that they are capable, therefore, of betrayal without qualm or quiver of guilt but also of inexplicable loyalty;
that they enjoy an occasional beating at the hands of their men; that
they are unforgiving and without charity to other members of their
own sex; that they lose keys and other small useful articles with mad-
dening regularity but are quite capable of finding things invisible to
men; that they use their sexuality with cold calculation to achieve their
inscrutable ends, etc., etc.

Until his last books, Faulkner treated with respect only females,
white ladies or colored women, past the menopause. The elderly
maiden or widowed aunt is the sole female figure in his fiction exempt
from travesty and contempt. Up to the very verge of her climacteric,
woman seems to Faulkner capable of the most shameless concupiscence,
like Miss Burden in *Light in August,* cowering naked in the garden of
the decaying house waiting to be captured and possessed in an obscene
game of hide-and-seek. Faulkner sometimes gives the impression of the
village misogynist swapping yarns with the boys at the bar in order to
reveal a truth about women which shocks even himself. Like old
Varner in *The Hamlet,* he keeps assuring his readers that he "cheer-
fully and robustly and undeviatingly" declines to accept "any such
theory as female chastity other than as a myth to hoodwink young hus-
bands. . . ." But there is little robust or cheerful about his attitudes,
however undeviatingly he may assert them; he is less like Varner fundamentally than like Hightower, the scared and stinking refugee from
life in *Light in August,* who cries out in despair that "the husband of
a mother, whether he be the father or not is already a cuckold . . .
what woman has ever suffered from any brute as men have suffered
from good women?"

Pubescent or nubile women, for Faulkner, fall into two classes,
roughly corresponding to those of Hemingway, though for the former
both are terrifying: great, sluggish, mindless daughters of peasants,
whose fertility and allure are scarcely distinguishable from those of a
beast in heat; and the febrile, almost fleshless but sexually insatiable

daughters of the aristocracy. Not the women he observes but those he dreams inhabit Faulkner's novels, myths of masculine protest: the peasant wench as earth goddess (Lena Grove in *Light in August,* Dewy Dell in *As I Lay Dying,* Eula Varner in *The Hamlet*), or the coed as nymphomaniac Venus (Cecily of *Soldiers' Pay,* Patricia in *Mosquitoes,* Temple Drake in *Sanctuary*). Their very names tend toward allegory, "Dewy Dell," for instance, suggesting both a natural setting and woman's sex, her sex as a fact of nature, while "Temple Drake" evokes both a ruined sanctuary and the sense of an unnatural usurpation: woman become a sexual aggressor—more drake than duck.

Unlike the natural women of Hemingway, Faulkner's dewiest dells turn out to be destroyers rather than redeemers, quicksands disguised as sacred groves. In his portrayal of Lena Grove, he relents for once into something like admiration; but his Eula Varner is more typical. Faulkner begins by describing Eula, the goddess who presides over the revels of *The Hamlet* and is married off in the end to its Devil, Flem Snopes, in terms of a pagan dithyramb to Aphrodite: "Her entire appearance suggested some symbology out of the old Dionysic Times, honey in sunlight and bursting grapes, the writhen bleeding of the crushed fecundated vine beneath the hard rapacious trampling goathoof." What begins as a pre-Christian eulogy to the inarticulate manifestation of sheer fertility imperceptibly slips over into a puritan cry of distress and distaste before unredeemed, burgeoning life.

Robert M. Slabey

The sex polarity in *Light in August* is most vividly detailed in three descriptions of Joe's "descent into the abyss"; each time the experience is twofold: first, the dark pit itself, followed by an awareness of its opposite, the street, thus making it possible to view their polarity in juxtaposition. Joe's first experience was at the age of fourteen with the Negro girl in the dark barn; he felt himself "enclosed by the womanshenegro"; (p. 137) leaning over her, "he seemed to look down into a black well and at the bottom saw two glints like reflection of dead stars." After the girl has fled his beating and he is engaged in fighting his comrades, there "was no She at all now . . . it was as if a wind

From "Myth and Ritual in Light in August*" by Robert M. Slabey,* Texas Studies in Literature and Language, *II (1960–61), 339–341. Excerpted and reprinted with the permission of the author and the publisher.*

had blown among them, hard and clean." Joe's terrifying night walk through Freedman Town (the Negro section) before he murders Joanna is related first in the anti-chronology of the novel and most fully. (pp. 99–101) He is enclosed by the cabinshapes and the women voices talking and laughing in a strange language: "It was as though he and all other manshaped life about him had been returned to the lightless hot wet primogenitive Female . . . It might have been the original quarry, abyss itself." Fleeing the "thick black pit," he ascends, panting and his heart thudding, into the main street and "the cool hard air of white people." During Joanna's nymphomania "It was as though he had fallen into a sewer"; (p. 224) "he was at the bottom of a pit in the hot wild darkness"; (p. 235) he "began to see himself as from a distance, like a man being sucked down into a bottomless morass." What he longed for was "the street lonely, savage, and cool." (pp. 227–228) The symbolic antithesis is between the images of the pit and the images of the breeze and the street, between female and male, wet, flaccid, hot darkness and dry, rigid, cool light. Pit and breeze are archetypes of female and male respectively: the pit is the primordial womb symbol; the procreative wind and the solar phallus symbolize the creative element in the source of the wind.

Joe rejects the Female on other occasions. An autoerotic assertion of his white masculinity is accomplished in a ritualistic fashion. Standing under Joanna's window he curses her "with slow and calculated obscenity," slashes the last button of his undergarment (recalling that a woman had sewed buttons on his clothes), walks naked across the yard feeling "the dew under his feet as he had never felt dew before." As he stands by the road in the thigh-tall weeds, the headlights of an approaching car shine on his body which becomes "white out of the darkness like a kodak print emerging from the liquid," and as the car passes a white woman shrieks. He spends the night in the deserted but still faintly ammoniac stable, thinking "It's because [horses] are not women. Even a mare horse is a kind of man." (pp. 93–95)

In contrast with these experiences there is the account of Joe's arrival at Miss Burden's in the spring—an earth ritual and a return to the womb. Lying in the copse, Joe can feel "the neversunned earth strike, slow and receptive, against him through his clothes" and is able to breathe in "the damp rich odor of the dark and fecund earth." (p. 199) Climbing through the kitchen window, he was "a shadow returning without a sound and without locomotion to the all-mother of obscurity and darkness." (p. 200) His early relations with Joanna are described in similar Freudian terms: "it had been as though he were outside a house where snow was on the ground, trying to get into the house." (p. 235) Joe's homosexuality has been accepted by several critics; his hermaphroditism (and there is a tradition that Adonis was a Hermaphrodite) is fundamentally psychic and his bisexual urges are symbolic of his opposing impulses. Freudian critics have been justified in citing as evidence the magazine which Joe reads—"of that type whose covers bear *either* pictures of women in underclothes *or* pictures of men in the act of shooting one another with pistols" (p. 96, *italics* added)—but they do not note the implications of an essentially indifferent correlative statement. They also fail to realize the strength of the comparative in Joe's thoughts on the McEacherns: "It was the woman: that soft kindness which he believed himself doomed to be forever victim of and which he *hated worse than* he did the hard and ruthless justice of men." (p. 147, *italics* added) Joe's revulsions at "womanfilth" and sex are balanced by his numerous anonymous promiscuities ("And always, sooner or later, *the street* ran through cities, through an identical and well-nigh interchangeable section of cities without remembered names, where beneath *the dark and equivocal and symbolical archways of midnight* he bedded with the women and paid them when he had the money, and when he did not have it he bedded anyway and then told them that he was a Negro"). (p. 196, *italics* added)

JOE CHRISTMAS: CHRIST FIGURE, VILLAIN, OR TRAGIC HERO

William Faulkner

Q. Mr. Faulkner, did you intend any Christ symbolism in *Light in August* in Joe Christmas?

A. No, that's a matter of reaching into the lumber room to get out something which seems to the writer the most effective way to tell what he is trying to tell. And that comes back to the notion that there are so few plots to use that sooner or later any writer is going to use some-

From Faulkner in the University, *ed. Frederick L. Gwynn and Joseph L. Blotner (Charlottesville: The University Press of Virginia, 1959), p. 117. Excerpted and reprinted with the permission of the publisher.*

thing that has been used. And that Christ story is one of the best stories that man has invented, assuming that he did invent that story, and of course it will recur. Everyone that has had the story of Christ and the Passion as a part of his Christian background will in time draw from that. There was no deliberate intent to repeat it. That the people to me come first. The symbolism comes second.

William H. F. Lamont

I believe that the desire to prove Joe Christmas to be a symbol of Jesus Christ has lured some scholars into assuming that Joe was the same age as Christ (thirty-three) at the time of his death. In the Introduction to the Modern Library edition of *Light in August,* Richard H. Rovere says: "There is Joe's uncertain paternity, the virginity of his mother, the spasmodic introduction of ideas of blood and sacrifice and crucifixion, and the fact that Christmas was lynched at the age Christ was when he was crucified" (xiii). The same kind of statement is made by Beekman W. Cottrell in the Winter 1956–57 *Modern Fiction Studies:* "There is the name of Joe Christmas, with its initials J. C. There is the fact of his uncertain paternity and his appearance at the orphanage on Christmas day. Joe is approximately thirty-three years of age at his lynching" (207).

William Faulkner himself tells us, however, that Joe was already thirty-three when he first arrived in Jefferson (197[1]) and that he lived there for three years. Therefore, he must have been thirty-six, not thirty-three, at the time of his death.

Furthermore, the mere addition of the number of years which Joe spent in different institutions and homes indicates that he was thirty-six when he died. He was an infant of three months when he was abandoned at the doorway of the home for foundlings (332, 335). He spent five years in the home (124). He spent thirteen years (from the ages of five to eighteen) on the farm of the McEacherns (180, 186). He spent the next fifteen years (from eighteen to thirty-three) drifting

From "The Chronology of Light in August," *by William H. F. Lamont,* Modern Fiction Studies, *III (1957–1958), 360–61. © 1958 by Purdue Research Foundation, Lafayette, Indiana. Reprinted with the permission of the publisher.*

[1] All page references are to the Modern Library edition of *Light in August.*

around the highways of the United States (195). He spent the last three years of his life (thirty-three to thirty-six) in Jefferson (81).

*   *   *

Limiting this brief note to the main facts of Joe's chronology, I think that I can safely say that as far as specific time references are concerned, Joe does not follow the Christ parallel at all. Joe was *not* born in December (Christmas) but in September; he was *not* crucified on a Friday (Good Friday), but on a Monday; he was *not* thirty-three when he died, but thirty-six.

William Faulkner

. . . Joe Christmas . . . didn't know what he was. He knew that he would never know what he was, and his only salvation in order to live with himself was to repudiate mankind, to live outside the human race. And he tried to do that but nobody would let him, the human race itself wouldn't let him. And I don't think he was bad, I think he was tragic. And his tragedy was that he didn't know what he was and would never know, and that to me is the most tragic condition that an individual can have—to not know who he was.

From Faulkner in the University, *ed. Frederick L. Gwynn and Joseph L. Blotner (Charlottesville: The University Press of Virginia, 1959), p. 118. Excerpted and reprinted with the permission of the publisher.*

John L. Longley, Jr.

—Aristotle has not defined pity and terror—said Stephen Dedalus—I have. Pity is the feeling which arrests the mind in the presence of whatsoever is grave and constant in human sufferings and unites it with the human sufferer. Terror is the feeling which arrests the mind in the presence of whatsoever is grave and constant in human sufferings and unites it with the secret cause.—

From The Tragic Mask: A Study of Faulkner's Heroes *by John L. Longley, Jr. (Chapel Hill: The University of North Carolina Press, 1963), pp. 192–204. Excerpted and reprinted with the permission of the publisher.*

It is appropriate that Joyce's Stephen Dedalus should formulate this definition, for, different as he is from Joe Christmas, they are alike in being heroes who are distinctly modern and who must make their way in a cosmos that is violent, chaotic, and absurd. Stephen's plight is only slightly less desperate than Christmas', and Stephen's motto *non serviam* is very close to Christmas' rigid determination not to submit to those forces that compulsively attempt to shape him to their will. . . .

Little else in modern literature has the speed and inevitable onward sweep of the chapter in which Percy Grimm pursues Christmas and kills him. Taken merely as evocative realism, the writing is superb: the shots, the shouting; the blind rushes and clotted confusion of the mob; the added detail of the fire siren, a characteristic sound of our time, screaming the rise and fall of its meaningless message; the early resolution of the pursuit into a personal contest between Christmas and Grimm. The rendition of Grimm as a type is as merciless as anything else of the sort ever done. Grimm is as the embodiment of pure force so often is: his rather colorless personality and appearance are in ghastly disproportion to his ability to produce evil and violence. He is Faulkner's equivalent of the classic Nemesis of the Furies— machine-like, unerring, impersonal, mindless. Here the problem of belief is no problem at all.

Still guided perhaps by his irrational hope, Christmas runs into Hightower's house holding the pistol he has snatched up on the way. He could kill Grimm easily, but with nothing to lose by another killing, he does not; this is his final gesture of human reconciliation. Grimm empties the magazine of his automatic into Christmas' body, but this is not all.

When the others reached the kitchen they saw the table flung aside now and Grimm stooping over the body. When they approached to see what he was about, they saw that the man was not dead yet, and when they saw what Grimm was doing one of the men gave a choked cry and stumbled back into the wall and began to vomit. Then Grimm too sprang back, flinging behind him the bloody butcher knife. "Now you'll let white women alone, even in hell," he said. But the man on the floor had not moved. He just lay there, with his eyes open and empty of everything save consciousness, and with something, a shadow, about his mouth. For a long moment he looked up at them with peaceful and unfathomable and unbearable eyes. Then his face, body, all, seemed to collapse, to fall in upon itself, and from out the slashed garments about his hips and loins the pent black blood seemed to rush like a released breath. It seemed to rush out of his pale body like the rush of sparks from a rising rocket; upon that black blast the man seemed to rise soaring into their memories forever and ever. They are not to lose it, in whatever peaceful valleys, beside whatever placid and reassuring streams of old age, in the mirroring faces of whatever children they will contemplate old disasters and newer hopes. It will be there, musing, quiet, steadfast, not fading and not particularly threatful, but of itself alone serene, of itself alone triumphant. Again from the town, deadened a little by the walls, the scream of the siren mounted toward its unbelievable crescendo, passing out of the realm of hearing.

They are not to lose it, nor, I think, are we. In Stephen Dedalus' terms, we feel pity and terror to a degree that is almost unbearable. One does not know why we feel these emotions or even less why the tragic spectacle is so compelling. It may be that it is better that we don't know. Certainly, as Nietzsche claimed, the tragic emotions lurk in the dark, irrational part of the blood, and very likely the rational mind wants no part of them. "Pity is the feeling which arrests the mind in the presence of whatsoever is grave and constant in human sufferings and unites it with the human sufferer." This part at least is no problem. We unite with Joe Christmas because he is the modern Everyman. In a cosmos where the only constants are absurdity and instability, we have the right to expect anything except rationality. Any one of us could become the victim. His suffering far transcends the time and place and means Faulkner has used and comes to stand for everything that is grave and constant in the human condition.

"Terror is the feeling which arrests the mind in the presence of whatsoever is grave and constant in human suffering and unites it with the secret cause." The union with the secret cause is almost as terrible as the suffering itself, because it gives a moment of true insight into ourselves. Part of this insight is perfectly symbolized in *Light in August* when the injured Hightower, in a scene that might have come straight out of Dostoyevsky, is working himself toward complete self-knowledge. As the wheel of his memory turns on and on, he comes to realize that his own cold selfishness, his absorption in the Confederate grandfather, has caused his wife's disgrace and death. As the crowd of faces in his memory struggles to come into focus, one of them becomes the dead face of Christmas, but the focus is not clear; another face is struggling with that face, struggling to become clear and be recognized. Suddenly it emerges: it is the face of Percy Grimm, gunman, mutilator, avenging fury, lyncher extraordinary. Hightower never saw either of them before the lynching, but their terrible failure and terrible guilt are somehow directly related to his own failure to live up to his humanity. Somewhere at the root of the secret cause of things as they are, we are all related; we are all involved. We are all responsible because we are all a part of mankind. So far as the rational mind goes, the union with the secret cause is a moment of awareness, of realizing that grave and constant human suffering is truly constant. Once we achieve this awareness, the acceptance of the tragic human situation, with all its absurdity and irrationality, becomes possible, and with the acceptance come the emotions of peace and tranquility.

LENA GROVE AND BYRON BUNCH

Irving Howe

Beyond a doubt Lena is the most harmoniously drawn character in the book. . . . But despite this elemental perfection, Lena is less interesting than Christmas or Hightower; she may indeed possess, as one critic writes, a "holistic consciousness" which shields her from the suffering of the other characters, but it remains a very limited sort of consciousness. So meager an intelligence must qualify, though not eliminate, our feeling for her. Those critics who see in Lena a triumph of traditional health and in Christmas the self-destructiveness of "modernism"—who see this and nothing else—do not really grant Faulkner's mind its due. . . . Is he not suggesting rather that Christmas and Hightower are destroyed because they accept, each in his inadequate way, the challenge of their humanity, the first by seeking selfhood and the second by a fanatical immersion in history, while Lena, the good unruffled vegetable Lena, survives them in her stupidity? Such a reading . . . invokes an observable truth: the price of effort often *is* self-destruction, and equally often the reward for animal calm is safety. One may be fond of Lena but one identifies with Hightower or, in a somewhat different way, with Christmas. To think of Lena as an agent of traditional morality is to graze the notion that goodness is contingent upon a low level of intelligence.

From William Faulkner: A Critical Study *by Irving Howe (New York: Random House, Inc., 1952), pp. 150–51. Copyright 1952 by Irving Howe. Excerpted and reprinted by permission of Random House, Inc.*

Walter J. Slatoff

The story of Lena Grove, with which the book begins and ends, has generally been seen as a pastoral frame for the novel, and Lena and Byron have usually been viewed as providing a norm of sanity and natural behavior against which the violence and perversions of the other stories can be measured. Certainly there is much to compel such a view. Lena's full-bodied health, serenity, and faith in the natural order of things, and her pleasure in life, are in sharp contrast to the fanaticism, barrenness, anguish, or despair that mark most of the other major characters. Hightower, "remembering the strong young body from out whose travail even there shone something tranquil and unafraid" thinks that she will have many more children—"*The good stock peopling in tranquil obedience to it the good earth; from these hearty loins without hurry or haste descending mother and daughter. But by Byron engendered next*" (p. 356)—and he goes on to suggest that obedience and relation to earth is perhaps equivalent to prayer. Byron, until the last chapter of the book at least, is clearly a norm, if not an ideal, of generosity and unpretentious decency, perhaps the most clearly virtuous of any of Faulkner's characters. His religion, unlike that of McEachern, Hines, and Hightower, is a peaceful modest affair; each Sunday he quietly and unobtrusively goes to a country church to lead the choir.

On the other hand, there is much which works in opposition to this view. Lena unquestionably has a kind of wisdom, but she is deeply mistaken about the character and intentions of Lucas, whose emptiness and falseness are completely and immediately apparent to everyone else who encounters him. When Mrs. Armstid warns her that Lucas will run away if she finds him, she answers, "I reckon a family ought to be all together when a chap comes. Specially the first one. I reckon the Lord will see to that" (p. 18). About this, too, she is terribly wrong, unless one is to consider as a being together the forced and brief encounter between Lena and Lucas just before he flees.

Numerous critics have seen Lena as a sort of earth-mother symbolizing the basic natural order, and Faulkner has said recently, "It was her

Reprinted from Walter J. Slatoff: Quest for Failure: A Study of William Faulkner, *pp. 175–78.* © *1960 by Cornell University. Excerpted and used by permission of Cornell University Press.*

destiny to have a husband and children and she knew it, and so she
went out and attended to it without asking help from anyone. . . .
She was never for one moment confused, frightened, alarmed." [1]
There is, however, another, far more trivial side to Lena. One of the
first things we learn about her is that on trips to town she would ask
her father to stop the wagon at the edge of town so she could walk
the rest of the way in "because she believed that the people who saw
her and whom she passed on foot would believe that she lived in the
town too" (p. 3). After breakfast at the Armstids she is very proud of
the fact that she "et polite." Nor is her treatment of Byron in the last
chapter particularly natural or admirable, especially when one remembers her easy acceptance and high valuation of the worthless Lucas.
Nor is it true that she was never for one moment confused, frightened,
or alarmed. She is distinctly confused and frightened by Mrs. Hines'
confusion and her own confusion about the identity of her child and
its father (p. 359), and she is very much alarmed when she believes
Byron has gone away for good. While it is true that she didn't ex-
plicity ask help from anyone, she is not unlike Anse Bundren in her
dependence on others and her expectation that help will be provided.
This expectation is not completely unself-conscious, Faulkner suggests
several times.[2]

It can be argued, of course, that without some of the characteristics
I have just pointed to Lena would lose all verisimilitude and become
pure symbol, much as Eula Varner is in *The Hamlet*. This is true, but
it is important to recognize these aspects of her character when one
proposes her as a norm or ideal.

But Faulkner undermines this view of her in a more important way
—by reducing her to a flat comic character at two crucial points in the
book. At the end of the first chapter as she approaches Jefferson, where
she hopes to find the father of her child, her only response is: "My,
my, . . . here I aint been on the road but four weeks, and now I am
in Jefferson already. My, my. A body does get around" (p. 26). And
at the very end of the book, after having tormented Byron terribly
with her apparent indifference to him, and seemingly unconcerned
about his clearly visible pain, she comments: "My, my. A body does
get around. Here we aint been coming from Alabama but two months,
and now it's already Tennessee" (p. 444).

[1] Jean Stein, "The Art of Fiction XII: William Faulkner," *Paris Review*, No. 12
(Spring, 1956), 50.
[2] See, for example, the description of the way she passes and notes the Armstid
wagon and then waits for it (pp. 6–10).

We are left finally, I think, with the kind of ambiguity about her which is suggested by the description of her face as having "either nothing in it, or everything, all knowledge" (p. 379), an ambiguity often encountered in Faulkner in the phrase "at once empty and profound."

Even harder to reconcile with the view of Lena and Byron as norm is the reduction of Byron in the last chapter to a purely comic character. Not only has he been presented as the highest representative of man and conscience throughout the book, but in the latter part he has grown in stature by taking more responsibility for the people around him than he ever had before. Moreover, more than any other character, he has been involved in all three stories. Yet in the final chapter Faulkner makes us see him chiefly as an ineffectual and ridiculous little man, so defeated and humiliated by Lena that the narrator of the section becomes "downright ashamed to look at him, to let him know that any human man had seen and heard what happened" (p. 441). It is true that both we and the narrator continue to feel sympathetic toward him, but we can hardly feel respect.

Norman Holmes Pearson

. . . Who is [Byron] Bunch? He is, as Faulkner describes him, "the kind of a fellow you wouldn't see at the first glance if he was alone by himself in the bottom of an empty concrete swimming pool." Looked at thematically, his is, as a student of mine once wrote, the situation of the great bunch (mass) of people who have not the tragic intensity of Joe, Joanna, or Hightower, but could follow their lead. We think of men like Byron Bunch in terms of where they place their loyalty. Bunch had believed that he could injure no man so long as he kept working at the lumberyard outside the city. His only social connection was with a parish in another town, which he left each week when Sunday was over. His nearest affinity was with Hightower, though he still stumbled when he entered Hightower's door. But when Byron first sees Lena he falls in love, completely and fully. His isolation is broken. He is sure of himself, he no longer stumbles, and he is ready to care for Lena and her unborn illegitimate child. He has found someone to belong to.

From The American Writer and the Feeling for Community, *by Norman Holmes Pearson, American Studies Inaugural Lecture, University of Alabama, March 20, 1962. Excerpted and reprinted with the permission of the author.*

When the book closes we see him and Lena and the child setting out again on an endless journey. The child is the future. Look at his heritage: he is a bastard by Burch, the foster son of Bunch, the godson of Hightower, and the apparent child of Joe Christmas (in the eyes of Joe's grandmother who would claim the baby for her own, and also of Lena who says, "and I think that his pa is that Mr.—Mr. Christmas too"). The nameless one is the heir of all these persons and of their solutions to life. He is a native of Jefferson. One remembers Joanna with her Calvin ancestry and the "white race's doom and curse for its sins." "The curse of every white child that ever was born and that ever will be born," her father said. "None can escape it." "Not even me?" Joanna asked. "And he said, 'Not even you. Least of all, you.'" Joanna speaks for the strain, when, in her words:

> I thought of all the children coming forever and ever into the world, white, with the black shadow already falling upon them even before they drew breath.

But yet this child of Lena is quiet at his mother's breast, and he is quiet because she is there with her timelessness and innocence, her repose in a troubled world of estrangement. He is a token of community. He, not Joe Christmas, is a Christ-child, related to all mankind. "A family ought to be together when a chap comes," a character has said early in the book, "Specially the first one. I reckon the Lord will see to that." The family is indeed now together, and is defined on the broader terms of the human community of all those who have willynilly, sinful or innocent, become involved.

And who is Lena? Hightower in his final scene remembers: "When he believed that he had heard the call it seemed to him that he could see his future, his life, intact and on all sides complete and inviolate, *like a classic and serene vase*, where the spirit could be born anew sheltered from the harsh gale of living and die so, peacefully, with only the far sound of the circumvented wind, with scarce even a handful of rotting dust to be disposed of." Joe Christmas vomits when the dietitian and the intern were in bed together. Later he again vomits when he learns from Bobbie about woman's "periodic filth": "In the notseeing and the hardknowing as though in a cave he seemed to see a diminishing *row of suavely shaped urns* in the moonlight, blanched. And not one was perfect. Each one was cracked and from each crack there issued something liquid, deathcolored and foul." Now, reminded of the classicly serene and suavely shaped urn as an ideal, we can remember with more symbolic significance the first description of Lena on her travels, seen at the beginning of the novel as we also see her at the end: "backrolling now behind her a long monotonous succession of peaceful and undeviating changes from day to dark and dark to day again, through which she advanced in identical and deliberate wagons as though through a succession of creakwheeled and limpeared avatars, *like something moving forever and without progress across an urn.*" It is Lena's progress in the book as though across the frieze of an urn, across the Grecian urn of Keats' poem, the endless line of the composed frieze, which having been contemplated, is "all ye know on earth, and all ye need to know."

> Thou still unravish'd bride of quietness,
> Thou foster-child of silence and slow time,
> Sylvan historian, who canst thus express
> A flowery tale more sweetly than our rhyme: . . .
> What men or gods are these? What maidens loth?
> What mad pursuit? What struggle to escape?
> What pipes and timbrels? What wild ecstasy?

Now, reflected from Keats' poem, we can see Lena Grove whose family name suggests the "leaf-fring'd legend." She is the "still unravish'd bride of quietness," the "foster-child of silence and slow time." Contrasted with her placid progress are the mad pursuit and the struggles of others to escape from social involvement. What struggling men or gods are these, we might indeed ask: what workmen, ne'er-do-wells, preachers, twisted similitudes of Christ? What way is offered against the egotistical ways of flight, vengeance, and withdrawal which destroy community? *Light in August* is the tale and the legend to serve as an example of the way of beauty and truth.

And what of Byron Bunch?

> Fair youth, beneath the trees, thou canst not leave
> Thy song, nor ever can those trees be bare;
> Bold lover, never, never canst thou kiss,
> Tho winning near the goal—yet, do not grieve;
> She cannot fade, tho thou hast *not* thy bliss,
> For ever wilt thou love, and she be fair!

The vision of the book and its established community is a final vision, "all breathing human passion far above." It is spiritualized. Yet it is evidenced on the basis of man's expressed relationship to man's fellow men.

GAIL HIGHTOWER

John L. Longley, Jr.

The usual flaw among [Faulkner's] tragic figures is pride, which quite often takes the form of insistence upon privilege or prerogative. . . .

The Reverend Gail Hightower's difficulties grow out of . . . concern with his own obsessions. His isolation from his fellow men and his denial of his responsibilities toward them grow out of his single-minded determination to have what he wants. What he wants is the right to live in Jefferson where his grandfather, a Confederate cavalryman, was shot dead from his horse in a raid. He is obsessed with the idea of the grandfather and is preoccupied with reconstructing an imaginary life built around the grandfather's accidental presence in Jefferson long ago. He has no real concern or interest other than being present at the window of his study late each afternoon when he imagines he hears the horses of the troop galloping through the town. His church members are bewildered and shocked by his concern with his grandfather, and his neglect of his wife drives her to nymphomania and eventually to a scandalous death. When he refuses to leave the town, he is taken into the woods by masked men and beaten unconscious. But he proves more stubborn than his attackers and in the long run the town decides to ignore him.

His one friend is Byron Bunch, and it is Byron who comes to Hightower and asks him to swear that Christmas was at Hightower's house the night of the murder. Hightower will not do it, even though it may save Christmas from the mob. "I've paid! I won't! I've bought immunity!" is his cry. Too late, when Percy Grimm is pursuing Christmas into Hightower's house, Hightower shouts out the lie that, told earlier, might have saved Christmas' life. But it comes too late, and Christmas is killed in Hightower's kitchen.

Later, when the violence is over and Hightower is going through an agonizing reappraisal of his life, he realizes that his own selfishness has brought on the death of his wife, that his own cowardice and his failure to save Christmas are somehow part and parcel of the guilt of

From The Tragic Mask: A Study of Faulkner's Heroes *by John L. Longley, Jr.* (*Chapel Hill: The University of North Carolina Press, 1963*), *pp. 227-29. Excerpted and reprinted with the permission of the publisher.*

Percy Grimm. In his arrogance, his selfishness and pride, his persistence in his line of conduct, and the fall from the high calling of his office, he is authentically tragic.

Carl Benson

What we have to deal with in *Light in August* is the peculiar collocation in Jefferson, Mississippi, of various lives whose stories cannot be accounted for on the basis of narrative alone. If, however, we see that the thematic conflict is between rigid patterns of self-involvement on the one hand and commitment to a solidarity that transcends self on the other, we must see that the chief character, the moral protagonist . . . is Gail Hightower, the old unchurched minister who is, as we open the story, ironically "Done Damned in Jefferson." It may be that at the end he is still damned as far as Jefferson is concerned, but through him the reader who inhabits a larger, though not dissimilar, community is enabled to estimate the relative moral worth of the other characters and the fixations which inhibit or limit their participation in society.

Actually, it might reasonably be argued that Hightower is also the central figure in a strict narrative sense and that far too many readers have been misled by the seemingly simple opposition of the violent Joe and the placid Lena. After all, Byron brings to Hightower the problems of Lena and Joe as well as his own. Joe's grandmother also comes to the old minister for assistance. Indeed, a good part of the action of the entire book seems designed to evoke the action or the response of Hightower. But it is his function of moral hero with which we are principally concerned. My argument is that he is a Yoknapatawpha Heyst who, like Conrad's hero, achieves a victory by traveling the moral distance from selfish immunity to redemption by the conviction that immunity cannot be bought. We have hints that his redemption is of major importance almost from the beginning. As soon as Byron Bunch brings him the problem of helping Lena, he breaks into a sweat of fear of being drawn from the isolation he thinks he had paid for. Thereafter, as Byron continues to ask his aid, though he replies, "I won't," and "I have paid," his compassionate nature

From "*Thematic Design in* Light in August," *by Carl Benson,* The South Atlantic Quarterly, *LIII (1954), 542–46. Excerpted and reprinted with the permission of the author and Duke University Press.*

gradually asserts its mastery; by the end he is so involved with "poor mankind" that he has delivered Lena's child and has tried to save Joe Christmas from Percy Grimm.

If it be objected that Hightower is no fit candidate for the role of moral hero, it may be said that Faulkner is aware of this irony, because he made it. Indeed, Faulkner's profound pessimism and his ultimate idealism both find witness in the use of Hightower as moral standard: pessimism, because we are given no better than Hightower as the slide rule for solidarity; idealism, because Hightower rises from the most foolish and inhumane illusion of all to tremendous heights by the abnegation of the illusion. He achieves moral stature in the only way possible for him—by descending into the pit of himself and ripping from his heart his dearest sin.

It is significant that Hightower's recognition of the true nature of his cherished illusion should be saved for the magnificent penultimate chapter . . . In this last scene we finally understand the childhood obsession that formed the original cause of his desire for immunity: the growing-up in a house populated by three phantoms (the sick mother, the harshly rigorous yet tame father, the old Negro woman) and a ghost, the heroic grandfather about whom the Negro woman told him stories, who was shot with a fowling piece while he was engaged in the very unmilitary, and yet somehow grand, prank of robbing a chicken coop. Brooding over this image of selfless, magnificent folly has caused the young Gail Hightower to become convinced that "I had already died one night twenty years before I saw light," and has compelled him to believe that "My only salvation must be to return to the place to die where my life had already ceased before it began." To this freakish illusion he has subordinated his entire life. . . . He uses the call to the ministry, the influences of the seminary and of his wife, to "shun the harsh gale of living," to get the pastorship in Jefferson, where his grandfather had died. Now, in his last revery as he sits dying . . . Hightower is finally beginning to see the enormity of his moral shortcomings . . . Here Faulkner introduces his effective turning-wheel imagery. Hightower's awakened moral consciousness turns slowly, like a wheel in heavy sand, as he unwillingly accepts the implications of his misspent life. . . . Thus, in the moment of final recognition, Hightower sees destroyed his cheating martyrdom, his justification for his behavior to his wife and the church, his immunity, and the cherished ghost itself.

In order to accentuate the significance of Hightower's moral struggle and victory, resulting in the abnegation of the illusion, Faulkner says,

"The wheel, released, seems to rush on with a long sighing sound. . . . It is going fast and smooth now, because it is freed now of burden, of vehicle, axle, all. In the lambent suspension of August [here perhaps is the moral significance of the title] into which night is about to fully come, it seems to engender and surround itself with a faint glow like a halo." The function of the wheel imagery shifts. The wheel is disengaged from the private conscience of Hightower and spins before him carrying on its circumference the faces of the people who have populated the novel. It is as if the old minister, freed at last of his morally debilitating illusion, has earned the right to pass judgment on the people he has ignored, misunderstood, or wronged. He sees all the chief figures of the novel and even some individually insignificant members of his congregation. And in the compassion he has attained by his acknowledgment of the ubiquity of human responsibility, he perceives that the faces of all suffering humanity are pretty much alike. . . .

Appendix: An Outline of the Narrative Structure of *Light in August*

by B. R. McElderry, Jr.

The Narrative Structure of Faulkner's Light in August

Day   *Ch. Forward Action*
               Immediate Past
               Remote Past

Day	Ch.	
Sat.	1	Lena's arrival in Jefferson. Burden fire sighted.
Sat.	2	Brown's association with Joe Christmas explained. Byron identifies Brown as Burch (Lena's seducer).
	3	Hightower's life in Jefferson. His wife's scandalous death. Loss of his church. His delivery of the Negro baby.
Sun.	4	Byron tells Hightower of Lena's search for Brown (Burch), of the fire, of the murder of Joanna Burden.
Fri.	5	Christmas quarrels with Brown, goes to town, returns: "Something is going to happen to me."
	6-7-8-9	Christmas at orphanage, adopted by McEacherns, meets waitress and tells her he is part Negro, beats up McEachern at dance, is himself beaten by waitress's friends.
	10	Christmas, three years before the murder, enters Joanna Burden's kitchen.

From "The Narrative Structure of Light in August," *by B. R. McElderry, Jr.,* College English, *XIX (1957–1958), 206–7. Excerpted and reprinted with the permission of the National Council of Teachers of English and B. R. McElderry, Jr.*

	11	Christmas seduces Joanna Burden.
		Story of the Burden family, abolitionists settled in the South.
	12	Christmas resents Joanna's increasing domination.
Fri.		Christmas murders Joanna when she draws a pistol.
Fri.		Christmas commandeers a car to further his escape.
Sat.	13	Sheriff investigates murder.
Tues.		Byron tells Hightower he is moving Lena to Brown's cabin at Burden Place.
Wed.		Hightower learns that Christmas's trail has been found.
Wed.		Hightower urges Byron to leave Lena.
Wed.	14	Deputy reports Lena staying at Brown's cabin.
Tues.		Christmas disturbs Negro church.
Fri. after murder		Christmas captured at Mottstown.
Fri.	15	Hineses learn of Christmas's capture.
Sun.	16	Through Byron, Mrs. Hines asks Hightower to give false alibi for her grandson, Christmas. Hightower refuses. Byron takes Hineses to Lena's cabin.
Mon.	17	Lena's baby born. Byron, previously refused by Lena, quits his job.
Mon.	18	Brown, taken by deputy to see Lena, escapes.
Mon.		Brown, pursued by Byron, beats him up.
Mon.		Byron learns Christmas has been killed.
Mon.	19	Lawyer Stevens puts Hineses on train, promising to send Christmas's body for burial.
Mon.		Christmas escapes, is shot and castrated by Percy Grimm.
	20	Hightower's early life—his Civil War father and grandfather, his invalid mother, his marriage to the minister's daughter.
Mon.		Hightower's death.
	21	The traveling furniture dealer's story of Byron's dog-like faithfulness to Lena, and her eventual acceptance of him.

Chronology of Important Dates

1918	April: Faulkner visits Phil Stone in New Haven. July: Faulkner leaves Oxford to begin training in the Royal Air Force in Toronto, Canada.	Henry Adams dies.
1919	Faulkner's "L'Après-Midi d'un Faune," appears in *The New Republic*. Faulkner enrolls in the University of Mississippi and works on *The Marble Faun*.	Sherwood Anderson, *Winesburg, Ohio*.
1920	Faulkner resigns from the University and goes to New York.	F. Scott Fitzgerald, *This Side of Paradise*; Ezra Pound, *Hugh Selwyn Mauberley*; Sinclair Lewis, *Main Street*; English translation of Freud's *A General Introduction to Psychoanalysis*.
1921	Faulkner returns to Oxford and becomes postmaster at the University.	
1922	Faulkner publishes a poem in *The Double Dealer*.	Marcel Proust dies. Eliot, *The Waste Land*; Joyce, *Ulysses*; E. E. Cummings, *The Enormous Room*.
1923		Harding dies and Coolidge becomes President. Wallace Stevens, *Harmonium*.
1924	*The Marble Faun* (poems), Faulkner's first book, published.	Nikolai Lenin, Woodrow Wilson, and Joseph Conrad die.
1925	Faulkner moves to New Orleans and begins association with *The Double Dealer* group, including Sherwood Anderson; writes *Soldiers' Pay*. July: sails for Europe. December: returns to Oxford.	Fitzgerald, *The Great Gatsby*; Theodore Dreiser, *An American Tragedy*; John Dos Passos, *Manhattan Transfer*; Ernest Hemingway, *In Our Time*.
1926	February: *Soldiers' Pay*, Faulkner's first novel, published.	Hemingway, *The Sun Also Rises*.

1927	April: *Mosquitoes.*	Publication of Proust's *A la recherche du temps perdu,* begun in 1908, completed.
1929	January: *Sartoris.* October: *The Sound and the Fury.* Faulkner marries Estelle Oldham and settles in Oxford.	Thomas Wolfe, *Look Homeward, Angel;* Hemingway, *A Farewell to Arms.* October: The Wall Street Crash.
1930	October: *As I Lay Dying.*	D. H. Lawrence dies. *I'll Take My Stand,* by "Twelve Southerners."
1931	February: *Sanctuary* revised and published. August: *Light in August* begun. September: *These Thirteen* (stories).	
1932	February: *Light in August* finished. May: Faulkner begins work in Hollywood. October: *Light in August* published.	Erskine Caldwell, *Tobacco Road.*
1933	April: *A Green Bough* (poems).	Nathanael West, *Miss Lonelyhearts;* W. B. Yeats, *Collected Poems.* Hitler becomes Chancellor of Germany; Roosevelt becomes President of the United States; Prohibition is repealed.
1934		Fitzgerald, *Tender Is the Night;* J. T. Farrell, *The Young Manhood of Studs Lonigan;* Henry Miller, *Tropic of Cancer.*
1935		Stevens, *Ideas of Order.*
1936	October: *Absalom, Absalom!*	
1938	February: *The Unvanquished.*	Thomas Wolfe dies. Dos Passos, *U. S. A.;* Allen Tate, *The Fathers.*
1939	January: *The Wild Palms.* Faulkner elected to the National Institute of Arts and Letters.	W. B. Yeats dies. John Steinbeck, *The Grapes of Wrath.* Italy invades Albania; Franco wins in Spain; Germany in-

		vades Poland; World War II begins.
1940	April: *The Hamlet.*	F. Scott Fitzgerald and Nathanael West die.
1941		United States enters World War II. James Joyce and Sherwood Anderson die.
1942	May: *Go Down, Moses.*	
1943		Eliot completes *Four Quartets.*
1945		Roosevelt dies and Truman becomes President; United States bombs Hiroshima and Nagasaki; World War II ends.
1946	April: *The Portable Faulkner,* edited by Malcolm Cowley.	Robert Penn Warren, *All the King's Men.*
1948	September: *Intruder in the Dust.* Faulkner elected to the American Academy of Arts and Letters.	Pound, *The Pisan Cantos;* Norman Mailer, *The Naked and the Dead.*
1949	November: *Knight's Gambit* (stories).	Robert Frost, *Complete Poems.*
1950	May: Faulkner awarded the Howells Medal for Fiction by the American Academy. August: *Collected Stories.* November: The Nobel Prize.	
1951	March: National Book Award for *Collected Stories.* September: *Requiem for a Nun.* October: Legion of Honor.	William Styron, *Lie Down in Darkness.*
1952		Ralph Ellison, *Invisible Man.*
1953		Saul Bellow, *The Adventures of Augie March.*
1954	August: *A Fable.*	Stevens, *Collected Poems.*
1955	National Book Award and Pulitzer Prize for *A Fable.* State Department trip to Japan.	Wallace Stevens and Thomas Mann die. Vladimir Nabakov, *Lolita.*

1957	Writer-in-Residence, University of Virginia. State Department trip to Greece. May: *The Town.*	
1958	Writer-in-Residence, University of Virginia.	Theodore Roethke, *Words for the Wind.*
1959	November: *The Mansion.*	
1961	State Department trip to Venezuela.	Ernest Hemingway dies.
1962	June 4: *The Reivers.* July 6: Faulkner dies in Oxford. July 8: Faulkner is buried.	E. E. Cummings dies.
1963		Robert Frost and Theodore Roethke die.
1965		T. S. Eliot dies.

Notes on the Editor and Contributors

DAVID L. MINTER teaches at Rice University. He has published essays on Jane Austen and F. Scott Fitzgerald and is the author of *The Interpreted Design*.

DARREL ABEL teaches at Purdue University. An Advisory Editor of *Modern Fiction Studies*, he is the author of several distinguished essays on American literature.

CARL BENSON teaches at Auburn University.

CLEANTH BROOKS teaches at Yale University. He is the author of several widely influential works, including *The Well Wrought Urn, Modern Poetry and the Tradition*, and *William Faulkner: The Yoknapatawpha Country*.

RICHARD CHASE formerly taught at Columbia University. His books include *Quest for Myth, Herman Melville, Emily Dickinson, Walt Whitman Reconsidered*, and *The American Novel and Its Tradition*.

MALCOLM COWLEY is a distinguished man of letters. He is the author of *Exile's Return, After the Genteel Tradition*, and *The Literary Situation*. In 1946 he edited *The Portable Faulkner*, a record of the compilation of which can be found in *The Faulkner-Cowley File: Letters and Memories, 1944–1962*.

LESLIE A. FIEDLER teaches at the State University of New York at Buffalo. A novelist and critic, he is the author of *Love and Death in the American Novel, No! In Thunder*, and *Waiting for the End*.

MAXWELL GEISMAR, a literary critic and historian, is the author of *Writers in Crisis, The Last of the Provincials, Rebels and Ancestors*, and other books.

IRVING HOWE teaches at Hunter College. He is the author of *Sherwood Anderson, Politics and the Novel, A World More Attractive*, and other books, as well as *William Faulkner: A Critical Study*.

WILLIAM H. F. LAMONT teaches at Rutgers, the State University, New Jersey, and has published articles and checklists in a number of American and European journals.

JOHN L. LONGLEY, JR., teaches at the University of Virginia. He is the author of *The Tragic Mask: A Study of Faulkner's Heroes.*

BRUCE R. MCELDERRY teaches at the University of Southern California. He is the author of essays on English and American literature of the nineteenth and twentieth centuries.

MICHAEL MILLGATE teaches at University College, University of Toronto. He is the author of *William Faulkner, American Social Fiction: James to Cozzens,* and *The Achievement of William Faulkner.*

WILLIAM VAN O'CONNOR formerly taught at the University of California at Davis. He wrote numerous essays and several books, including *The Tangled Fire of William Faulkner.*

NORMAN HOLMES PEARSON teaches at Yale University. He edited, with William Rose Benét, the *Oxford Anthology of American Literature,* and with W. H. Auden, *Poets of the English Language,* and he has written many essays on American literature of the nineteenth and twentieth centuries.

ROBERT M. SLABEY teaches at the University of Notre Dame. He is the author of several essays on modern literature.

WALTER J. SLATOFF teaches at Cornell University. He is the author of *Quest for Failure: A Study of William Faulkner.*

LAWRANCE THOMPSON teaches at Princeton University. He is the author of *Fire and Ice: The Art and Thought of Robert Frost, Melville's Quarrel with God,* and *William Faulkner: An Introduction and Interpretation.*

OLGA W. VICKERY teaches at the University of Southern California. She is co-editor of *William Faulkner: Three Decades of Criticism* and is the author of *The Novels of William Faulkner: A Critical Interpretation.*

HYATT H. WAGGONER teaches at Brown University. He is the author of *The Heel of Elohim, Hawthorne,* and *William Faulkner.*

Selected Bibliography

In addition to the essays by Alfred Kazin and John L. Longley mentioned in the Editor's Introduction and to the fuller original texts of the essays and excerpted statements included in this collection, the reader will find useful the following:

Backman, Melvin. *Faulkner: The Major Years.* Bloomington: Indiana University Press, 1966, pp. 67–87. A general study useful especially for its study of Gail Hightower.

Chase, Richard, "The Stone and the Crucifixion: Faulkner's *Light in August,*" *Kenyon Review,* X (1948), 539–51. A perceptive study of several important patterns of imagery.

Hirshleifer, Phyllis, "As Whirlwinds in the South: An Analysis of *Light in August,*" *Perspective,* II (1949), 225–39. Particularly useful for its discussion of religious and sexual motifs.

Holman, C. Hugh, "The Unity of Faulkner's *Light in August,*" *PMLA,* LXXIII (1958), 155–66. A thorough but unsatisfactory examination of the relationship between the Passion Story and *Light in August.*

Kirk, Robert W., "Faulkner's Lena Grove," *Georgia Review,* XXI (1967), 57–64. A useful study to compare with Howe, Slatoff, and Pearson in this collection.

Lind, Ilse Dusoir, "The Calvinistic Burden of *Light in August,*" *New England Quarterly,* XXX (1957), 307–29. One of the fuller treatments of religious motifs, and particularly of Southern "Puritanism" or "Calvinism," in *Light in August.*

Nemerov, Howard, "Calculation Raised to Mystery: The Dialectics of *Light in August,*" in *Poetry and Fiction: Essays,* pp. 246–59. New Brunswick, New Jersey: Rutgers University Press, 1963. An essay interesting particularly with regard to Faulkner's technique.

Pearson, Norman Holmes, "Lena Grove," *Shenandoah,* III (1952), 3–7. An earlier version of the essay reprinted in this collection, but with more exclusive focus on Lena Grove and the urn imagery.

Slabey, Robert M., "Joe Christmas, Faulkner's Marginal Man," *Phylon,* XXI (1960), 266–77. An interesting essay to compare with Longley's treatment of Joe Christmas in this collection.

West, Ray B., Jr., "Faulkner's *Light in August:* A View of Tragedy," *Wisconsin Studies in Contemporary Literature,* I (1960), 5–12. An important treatment of *Light in August* as basically tragic in mode.